T: ROBERT FROST:
Farm-Poultryman

The story of Robert Frost's career
as a breeder and fancier of hens
& the texts of eleven long-forgotten
prose contributions by the poet, which appeared
in two New England poultry journals
in 1903-05, during his years of farming
at Derry, New Hampshire

Edited by

EDWARD CONNERY LATHEM
& **LAWRANCE THOMPSON**

Dartmouth Publications
HANOVER · NEW HAMPSHIRE · 1963

THE STINEHOUR PRESS · LUNENBURG · VERMONT

Contents

7   *Introduction*

31   Trap Nests

37   A Just Judge

45   A Start in the Fancy

52   The Question of a Feather

60   Old Welch Goes to the Show

67   The Original and Only

73   Three Phases of the Poultry Industry

84   The Cockerel Buying Habit

88   "The Same Thing Over and Over"

93   The Universal Chicken Feed

98   Dalkins' Little Indulgence

107   *Editors' Notes*

Introduction

ROBERT FROST liked to recall that in his early days, before he had won recognition as a poet, he had experimented with many possible occupations. Given the proper encouragement, he would reminisce engagingly on the diversity of those adventures. To interested journalists he might, for example, describe his experiences as a newsboy on the streets of San Francisco, or his work as contributor to his high school paper in Lawrence, Massachusetts, or his later periods of employment as a cub reporter. Teachers sometimes heard him tell of his beginnings in pedagogy: of how he "ran away" from Dartmouth to restore discipline among the unruly boys in an eighth-grade class his mother was, with difficulty, trying to handle; of how in taking over his mother's position he walked into that classroom on the first day with a fixed determination and brandishing menacingly a handful of rattans. Factory workers or union officials were apt to stir his recollections of life in a textile mill— memories that included the awful time when a broom he dropped from a ladder, high above, had gone ripping through the threads of a jackspool, cutting every strand.

He also liked to tell of his one, ill-fated venture as an impresario; of how, while still in his teens, he had answered a newspaper ad and thus become the manager— for the duration of but a single, disillusioning engage-

7

ment—of a Shakespearean reader of the old-style elocu-
tionist cast. Among his lesser adventures he could make
mention, too, of the summer he had spent tending a fish
weir near one of the big dams on the Merrimack at Lawrence, or of his brief time as a budding conchologist, as-
signed the task of wrapping and labeling sea shells for a
collector who had hired him—and soon fired him, because he spent too much time admiring, and satisfying
his scholarly curiosities about, the univalves and bivalves
he was being paid to sort.

Always entertaining and usually humorous in these
reminiscences, Frost occasionally concluded such anec-
dotes by telling, whimsically, that he had once been a
piece-worker in a shoe factory at Salem, New Hampshire,
where he had performed the function of inserting nails
into holes in heels that were about to be attached to nearly
finished shoes; that in the interest of speeding up pro-
duction he had always held a supply of nails in his mouth
as he worked; and that any success he had attained in
later life could properly be attributed to the fact that he
had neither swallowed nor inhaled too many of those
little nails.

One boast Robert Frost could make, but which he
rarely did make, was that he had seriously devoted several years of his early life to the raising of hens which were
"bred to lay." That little-known chapter in the Frost
story began as a result of doctor's orders, given him in
the spring of 1899. Twenty-five years old and fresh from
giving up college studies for a second time, he was already a married man with the beginnings of a family, act-
ing as an assistant in a private school then being carried
on by his mother in Lawrence. Never robust, he was at

this period troubled intermittently by peculiar pains across the lower part of his chest, and he had sought the advice of several doctors concerning the possible cause. Finally, one physician who was consulted learned that Frost's father had died of consumption at the age of thirty-four, and this information led to a suspicion that the son too might be suffering from tuberculosis. Accordingly, the doctor urged him to find work out of doors, preferably on a farm.

Although city-born and pretty completely city-bred, Robert Frost knew enough about farming to be quite certain he could never tolerate its drudgery. But, as he cast about for alternatives, he remembered that on some of his walks into the countryside around Lawrence he had seen and admired a large, well-kept poultry farm in the adjacent town of Methuen, Massachusetts. It was possible, he thought, that poultry farming might be a bearable, perhaps even a pleasant, way of meeting the doctor's orders. Actually, he could claim that he had, in a sense, already passed through a part of his apprenticeship in this branch of husbandry, for during his boyhood days in San Francisco a friend had given him and his younger sister a few newly hatched chicks as pets. Young Robbie had been fascinated by the fluffy creatures; and he had tended them and raised them with care and pride in the back yard of their home on Leavenworth Street.

He decided to explore further the possibilities that might now exist for him in the realm of poultry raising by visiting the big Methuen farm. Its owner proved to be a French-Canadian who bore up proudly under the name of Charlemagne Bricault. Indeed, he was "Doctor Bricault," a veterinarian by profession. Currently his specialty was the breeding of supposedly pedigreed birds, Barred Plymouth Rocks and White Wyandottes, with particular emphasis apparently on the latter. "Bred to lay" was the slogan of the Bricault Poultry Farm, whose birds were, its advertisements regularly proclaimed, "Carefully bred from dams of standard weight, whose egg laying record for each succeeding generation was individually known to have increased from year to year. Males are all from 200-egg hens." The price per sitting of fifteen Bricault Farm eggs, $1.50.

Frost was impressed with what he saw and what he was told. Moreover, the Doctor promptly suggested that if his visitor would really like to start a brood of Wyandottes himself, he would gladly supply him eggs for incubation and, later on, would be glad to help with the marketing of Frost's own eggs and poultry as they became available. It seemed a handsome offer.

During the next few weeks, in the spring of 1899, Frost, his mind made up to enter upon this new enterprise, found what seemed to be a suitable location, and he rented one side of a house, well out in the country, near the New Hampshire boundary line in the town of Methuen—not very far, as a matter of fact, from the Bricault farm. As soon as he had settled his family into their new home, he busied himself with the building of hen houses. When at last all was ready, he arranged to have Doctor Bricault deliver enough eggs to fill two large incubators. Thus, in a short space of time, the former teacher, millhand, reporter, factory worker, and doer of odd jobs became a farm-poultryman.

Within a year, Frost decided that he must have more space. A search ensued, and at length an attractive twenty-acre farm was located, not too many miles away, in Derry, New Hampshire. At his wife's urging, he obtained help from his grandfather Frost, who purchased the little farm for him—on the condition, however, that Rob would bind himself to the place for at least ten years. (All of the grandson's earlier experiments with so great a variety of occupations had caused suspicion and doubt on the grandfather's part.) Title to the property was, therefore, to be held in William P. Frost's name, but with the understanding that the property would be Rob's at the end of ten years' time. The terms were accepted, and in the autumn of 1900, Frost moved with Mrs. Frost and their year-old daughter, Lesley, to the farm at Derry, as was duly recorded in the columns of a local paper, *The Derry News*, on October 5, 1900:

R. Frost has moved upon the Magoon place which he recently bought. He has a flock of nearly 300 Wyandotte fowls.

The farm was an idyllic retreat. Its small and relatively new house was conveniently connected to shed and barn. Orchards, gardens, and hayfields surrounded the modest set of buildings, with a woodlot and two good pastures nearby. The former owner had worked for years in a fruit nursery and had thus been led to improve the farm with several small but choice orchards. Its apple trees included in their varieties Gravensteins, Northern Spies, and Baldwins. There were smaller groves of peach, pear, and quince. A patch of cultivated raspberry bushes flourished behind the barn. And most important of all there was plenty of room for the new occupant's hens to run, with little need for special fencing.

11

During the first two or three years, the Frosts made few friends at Derry. Their only regular caller was the indefatigable Charlemagne Bricault. Although he left Methuen at the end of 1900 to manage for several months a farm at Woodstock, Vermont, he soon returned and re-established his business in nearby Andover, Massachusetts. Bricault picked up Frost's fresh eggs, took away crates of live "broilers" and "roasters," and bought cockerels for resale to other farmers interested in systematic breeding. And all the while he kept encouraging his novice friend with advice and reassurances: no other branch of farming paid nearly so well as the poultry business, he said.

As he recovered his health and grew stronger, Frost threw himself into the work with increased gusto. He followed newspaper accounts of market prices. He read attentively the columns of poultry magazines. He made trips to poultry shows in the area, particularly those at Amesbury, Massachusetts. He even looked forward to the day when he himself might exhibit a prize-winning bird which could be sold for a huge profit.

None of these preoccupations made Robert Frost forget, however, the literary aspirations which had long been developing in him. To be sure, the poems he had written since moving to Derry—surreptitiously and late at night, beside the kitchen stove—had seemed to make little appeal to the magazine editors to whom they were occasionally sent. But becoming, as time went on, more knowledgeable in poultry matters, he finally hit upon the idea of extending his literary efforts from poetry to a specialized kind of prose which would reflect his new vocation. It seemed to him that if he were to turn his hand to prose fiction, and particularly to stories about poultry or matters associated with the trials and triumphs of the world of poultry, he might possibly be able to produce some informative and entertaining sketches. Perhaps, indeed, he could persuade the poultry editors that this novel kind of reading fare deserved a place in their publications.

Cautiously he sent off a query to *Farm-Poultry*, a well-known semi-monthly journal in Boston, founded more than a decade earlier to constitute "A Practical Farm and Suburban Poultry Raising Guide." As the editor later had occasion to recall, what was proposed by the would-be author from Derry was "articles a little out of the usual line, but with instructive ideas in them." *Farm-Poultry* was "always ready to investigate anything offering possibilities of good copy," and Frost was invited to forward a sample piece for consideration. "He did so, and," the editor reported candidly in retrospect, "we didn't like it a bit; sent it back."

Although he failed utterly in his approach to *Farm-Poultry*, Frost was more successful, as it proved, with a rival publication, *The Eastern Poultryman*, a monthly then being issued at Freeport, Maine. At least three prose sketches were submitted to *The Eastern Poultryman*, for three were accepted and published by the magazine. The first, signed simply with the initials R. L. F., is discovered in the issue for February, 1903. Its title, "Trap Nests," referred, as readers of *The Eastern Poultryman* could be expected to know, to a type of nest so constructed that a hen upon entering it cannot leave until she is released: a device useful for keeping an accurate record of the egg-laying of each individual bird. An editorial comment on "The Trap Nest Story" also appeared in this same number. Expressing confidence that the contribution would "interest and amuse our readers," the editor went on to observe that, "The experiences of Mr. and Mrs. Aiken" (the thwarted and discouraged characters of Frost's story) "are similar to those met by many others who look upon the poultry business as one in which no skill or knowledge is required, and so venture in without any preparation, and later find to their sorrow that 'things are not what they seem.' " Continuing with a paragraph of sympathetic remarks on the use of trap nests, the commentary concluded with the observation, "We trust our readers will understand the story in the spirit in which its author intended, and that like Mr. Aiken they may look for 'results' as being of as much importance as following a method of feeding or management that may seem popular whether it is based upon science, common sense or the caprice or greed of its originators."

There followed in the March *Eastern Poultryman* the second R. L. F. story, entitled "A Just Judge." Then, four months later, the third was published. This final contribution was called "A Start in the Fancy," and, as every subscriber, again, would be aware, "the fancy" referred to that aspect of poultry interest concerned with fine stock, including the keeping of birds primarily or exclusively for exhibition or other non-commercial purpose.

If the editor of *Farm-Poultry* had seen no merit in the article sent by Frost to his own magazine, he was not slow to recognize the quality of what he soon found published by a competitor. The initial *Eastern Poultryman*

14

piece evidently escaped his notice, but he saw the second and pronounced it "a very interesting story." It was, moreover, he thought, "in a style somewhat familiar." And he recorded further, "We couldn't place it at first, but later recalled that the initials were those of that correspondent whose story weighted with information had been returned." Arrangements were made forthwith for reprinting "A Just Judge" in *Farm-Poultry*. This was done in the issue for May 1, 1903, and, as the editor subsequently reported to his readers, he had also written off hopefully to Mr. Robert L. Frost of Derry, urging that "if the story in the *Eastern Poultryman* was his to send us what plain stories he had, and we would make him an offer for any we could use."

Of the manuscripts Frost now submitted to *Farm-Poultry*, three were immediately accepted and were published during that summer of 1903. "The Question of a Feather" was featured on the first page of *Farm-Poultry* for July fifteenth. Next, "Old Welch Goes to the Show" was published in mid-August; and just two weeks later, on September first, came the third story, "The Original and Only." Others soon followed. In all, over a period of two and a half years, a total of nine contributions (including the *Eastern Poultryman* reprint) by Robert Lee Frost appeared in the Boston magazine. The pieces ranged in length from nine hundred to three thousand words, and all but one were signed simply with the author's initials: R. L. F. Each of these early prose sketches in *The Eastern Poultryman* and *Farm-Poultry* subtly reflects actions and voice-ways characteristic of New England farmers. Some of them contain, too, distinct elements of that typically Frostian flavor and tone which, a decade later, were so prominently associated with the *North of Boston* eclogues.

In his venture as prose-writing poultryman, Frost made one mistake that was to cause him some little embarrassment. It occurred in the only straight piece of reporting that he did for the pages of *Farm-Poultry*: an article on three praiseworthy examples of poultry-farming conducted there in the region just south of Derry. He began the article, published in the number for December 15, 1903, by describing Doctor Bricault's White Wyandotte farm in Andover, Massachusetts. Then he extended the account by lauding the initiative of a Lawrence carpenter who had grown tired of city life and had bought six acres in the countryside near the village of Salem, New Hampshire. Saving the best for last, Frost concluded the piece with an account of a small but picturesque farm owned by the equally picturesque John A. Hall, in the town of Atkinson, New Hampshire. Hall was, as Frost described him, a small breeder who "in addition to White Wyandottes . . . indulges a taste for several varieties of ducks and geese, not to mention Runt pigeons and Angora cats on the side."

It was inevitable that the best of the accounts in this exposition of "Three Phases of the Poultry Industry" should in fact have been the one devoted to Hall. He was a figure well known in the region for his oddities. Frost had made his acquaintance at an Amesbury poultry show, and the two men had quickly become friends and arranged to exchange visits. When Frost first drove his buggy down to Atkinson to pay his promised call, he discovered Hall's house and barn tucked in off the road, beyond a brook cluttered with ducks and geese. The barnyard sheltered a surprising congregation of plain and fancy birds. The whole picture was as quaint as a scene by Currier and Ives. Inside the farmhouse were further surprises: John Hall was not married, but he lived in relative peace and comfort with a common-law housekeeper-wife and her mother.

The mistake of consequence, made by Frost in his reporting the activities of John Hall, had nothing to do of course with the domestic arrangements of the Hall household. It was, rather, a purely technical blunder—that of letting his imagination supplement his knowledge in the following passage:

Two things in breeding he makes of first importance—size and vigor. It is his experience that weight tends constantly to decline. It is a simple matter to keep it up, only it cannot be left to take care of itself. As for vigor, it is easier to get this right than not. What the stock need is a little judicious neglect. Mr. Hall's geese roost in the trees even in winter. Such a toughening process would be too drastic for hens, but these have to take it according to their strength.

More than one north-of-Boston farmer must have chuckled at the reference to geese roosting in trees. Perhaps more than one subscriber to *Farm-Poultry* wrote in to ask questions. One mildly sarcastic query was, at any rate, published in the issue for January 15, 1904, in the form of a letter from H. R. White of Doylestown, Massachusetts:

Editor FARM-POULTRY:—Will you kindly inform me through your next issue what kind of geese Mr. Hall has that Mr. R. L. Frost speaks of in your issue of Dec. 15th? According to Mr. Frost these geese roost in the trees even in the win-

17

ter time. Now I am 45 years old and have been among geese all my life time, and I can never remember seeing a goose in a tree. I thought if I could get a breed of that kind I could dispense with coops.

Mr. White's letter was printed under the caption, "It's 'Up to' Mr. Frost," and the editor, by way of a postscript, added his own comment:

Letting Mr. Frost's statement pass is one "on" us. The writer's attention was called to the evident error before the paper was mailed, but too late to make correction. Then we thought we'd wait and see how many would notice it. Mr. Frost will have to explain.

Explain he did, as best he could and by trying to make a little joke out of his regrettable slip. In the process of his joking, however, he unhappily compounded his difficulty by committing yet another mistake. His answer appeared in the issue for February 15, 1904:

Editor FARM-POULTRY:—In reply to Mr. White's (and yours) of recent date in regard to the error in the article on Mr. Hall's place, there is this to say:—
Geese would sleep out, or float out, let us say, where hens would roost in the trees. To be sure. But what more natural, in speaking of geese in close connection with hens, than to speak of them as if they *were* hens? "Roost in the trees," has here simply suffered what the grammarians would call attraction from the subject with which it should be in agreement to the one uppermost in the mind. That is all. But the idea will have to stand, viz., that Mr. Hall's geese winter out,— and that is the essential thing. Mr. White is not after geese that roost in the trees, but geese that don't need coops. Well, Mr. Hall has them that prefer not to use coops, whether they

need them or not. My impression is that he has them in several varieties, and I'll risk my impression. But Mr. Hall is a good fellow and will be glad to tell Mr. White about his geese himself—doubtless, also, to do business with him.

This time the magazine did not wait to see how many of its readers might notice the new error by which the author-poultryman from Derry had now unintentionally heightened the awkwardness of his posture. Instead, the editor appended his own gentle corrective immediately below the Frost letter, together with some attractive details of explanation:

Mr. Frost seems not to be aware of the fact that geese generally remain out of doors by choice practically all the time. The same thing may be said of ducks. My Indian Runner ducks (now deceased) would stay out in a snow storm from daylight to dark rather than go into a comfortable shed where they were well sheltered and amply provided with bedding. If anyone will watch the actions of the duck or goose when out in the snow, and will consider that the feet are the only parts requiring protection, he will readily understand how they can be seemingly so indifferent to the weather.

Water fowl do not sit with their feet on the snow. They lie flat on their bellies, draw their feet up to their sides, and then with a few dextrous wiggles work the feet into the feathers where they are warm and comfortable. I think that average hardy fowls will do this by preference rather than remain under shelter.

These observations could have concluded the knowing laughter which probably went the rounds at Frost's expense. Unfortunately, however, before his own letter (with this unexpected editorial comment and correction) appeared, Frost had decided it might be well to protect himself further by having John Hall write a letter in his defense. But, as all his friends and enemies knew, John Hall had had little schooling, and his talents did not include epistolary abilities. The best he could do was to enter into collusion with his friend by giving approval to a letter actually composed by Frost. The letter appeared in the issue of *Farm-Poultry* for March 1, 1904, under the caption, "Geese Don't Roost, but Some Ducks Do":

Editor FARM-POULTRY:—I noticed Mr. H. R. White's letter in your paper asking about the kind of geese I keep that sleep out in the winter. They are Toulouse, Embden, and Buff. They don't roost in trees. I don't know how Mr. Frost made that mistake, for of course he knows better.

We have often talked about the way they take to the water at night, a favorite place for them to hang up being on a stone just under water. A good many nights in winter, as well as in summer, I have no idea where they are; and I think they are better every way out doors as long as there is any water not frozen over. But speaking of geese in trees, I don't suppose Mr. White has ever seen a duck in a tree. I have. And I once had a duck that laid her eggs in a tree high enough to be out of reach from the ground, and brought off twenty-two ducklings. These were Brazilians, and I don't know what they won't do.

It has always seemed strange to me how people succeed in keeping geese shut up. If I shut mine up they begin to be restless right away, and go off in looks, especially plumage. Mr. White needn't think because I let my geese run wild I think any less of them than other folks. They are good ones, —as they ought to be with the advantages I give them. They win, too, where they are shown.

The records in your paper ought to show what they did in Lawrence this year; but I notice they don't. So Mr. Frost was pretty near right about my geese; and if Mr. White wants some good ones that a little rather than not sleep out, I've got them.

The exchange had gone far enough, and this letter was printed without comment. But Frost, somewhat embarrassed and self-conscious, apparently slacked off his literary contributions on the subject of poultry. Before the trouble broke he had, however, already contributed additional narratives. *Farm-Poultry* for February 1, 1904, which appeared between the issues that had, respectively, carried White's dry challenge and Frost's limping answer, contained another sketch or short story by Frost titled "The Cockerel Buying Habit." The issue of March 1, 1904, which had published the letter written by Frost but attributed to John Hall, also carried a sketch by Frost entitled (with unintentional irony) " 'The Same Thing Over and Over.' " On April 1, 1904, came "The Universal Chicken Feed." Then there was a long silence for more than a year and a half, until on December 15, 1905, *Farm-Poultry* carried on its first page Frost's final contribution to the periodical. It was called "Dalkins' Little Indulgence—A Christmas Story."

At about the time his last contribution to *Farm-Poultry* had been published, Robert Frost was beginning to ease himself out of hen-raising in particular and out of farming in general (although as late as 1908 he remained enough of a poultryman to become one of the directors of the newly organized Derry Poultry Association). During the autumn of 1906 he became a regular member of the faculty at Derry's Pinkerton Academy, where he

21

continued teaching for five years. Following this, in 1911, he left for Plymouth with Pinkerton's principal, Ernest L. Silver, who had accepted appointment as head of the New Hampshire State Normal School there. For a single year, Frost taught psychology and the history of education at Plymouth Normal. Then he made up his mind that he was willing to gamble once again on a career in writing. Selling the farm in Derry, he took his family to England in the fall of 1912, and within a few months he had found a publisher in London for a volume of his poetry. Late in 1913, even while *A Boy's Will* was being acclaimed, and not long before *North of Boston* was published, Frost, with the beginnings of his fame looming brightly on the horizon, wrote self-deprecatingly from England to his friend Ernest Silver, back in New Hampshire:

At most poetry can pave the way for prose and prose may or may not make money. I have still the battle all before me and with not much stomach for the money-making part of it. I am less inclined to prose than I thought I was when I looked into the future out of a normal school window in Plymouth. I was always that way. Two or three days on end I would write prose, first having resolved it was the thing for a man with a family to do. But just when I thought I bade fair to produce a novel, right in the middle of chapter three or four I would bring up in another inconsequential poem. Sort of incorrigible I am. Once I actually did write some half dozen short stories I sold to Farm Poultry (Boston) for ten dollars apiece. That was about as far as I ever got.

Thus he referred to and dismissed his contributions of prose to *Farm-Poultry*. Yet, while still in England he had also had, as it happened, special occasion to invoke them for the purpose of admonishing one of his former Pinkerton students on an important point in the art of newspaper reporting. The student, John T. Bartlett, had shown at the Academy ability as a writer, and Frost had encouraged him to continue. The two, teacher and pupil, became devoted friends and kept in touch with one another after Bartlett married and became a reporter in Vancouver, British Columbia. In a letter to Frost, written early in 1913, Bartlett had apparently confessed that he had got himself into journalistic difficulties by giving too much play to his own fancy in describing a picturesque character known as "Biblical Smith." In his answer, Frost gently reprimanded Bartlett:

You mustn't fake articles any more. Not even in details. Them's orders. I'll tell you why. It's taking an unfair advantage. Of whom? Of the public? Little I care for them. They would deceive themselves were there no one else to deceive them. Of your fellow journalists then? I suspect that they can hold up their end. No it is taking an unfair advantage of the gentlemen who profess fiction. I used to think of it when I faked in a small way for another paper named the Sun which was published in Lawrence Mass. All I had to do was to claim for my yarns the virtue of fact and I had story writers of twice my art and invention skun a mile. I thought of it again when partly for the fun and partly for the lucre I tried my hand at poultry journalism. I wrote up one or two poultrymen as you did Biblical Smith filling in the gaps in my knowledge with dream material. I think I managed fairly well except for the time I spoke of John Hall's geese roosting in the trees. I should have let geese severely alone. It took an artistic letter from John Hall himself (I wrote it for the douce man) to save me from the scandal that started. I had a little right on my side. As a matter of fact John Hall had among others a few Brazilians that sometimes roosted on a pollared willow and even on the chimney and he could honestly say so (if some one would write the letter for him, for he was without clerkly learning.) But I was uncomfortable all the time until I settled back to write out-and-out stories. It had occurred to me previously that some fiction not purporting to be true otherwise than as fiction is true, true to the life of the farm and especially the poultry farm wouldn't derogate from the serious not to say solemn interest of a poultry journal. I succeeded in creating a limited demand for it and was making a very little money when I decided I could make more in Pinkerton. I tell you all this to show you. A little faking in our salad days is none so sinful—a novice naturally takes it as a lark—he can't feel that he has tasted the full flavor of the world the flesh and his grown-up-mans job if he hasn't tried it. But you will soon sicken of it, if you havent sickened already.

After the play of imagination in poetry had become for Robert Frost the predominant preoccupation, he continued to blend with it a disciplined attention to realistic fact and detail. Those familiar with his poetry and aware of his years devoted to poultry raising cannot fail to notice the occasional glimpses of images and circumstances which combine poetic truths about hens and actual experience with their hopeful care and breeding. One *North of Boston* poem entitled "The Housekeeper" reaches back, for example, for its setting and characterization to the farm of John Hall of Atkinson, and to certain of the problems of that poultryman-farmer, as the following extract of dialogue reveals. The first speaker would seem to be John Hall's mother-in-common-law, and the second speaker might be the poet himself as visitor:

24

"Our hens and cows and pigs are always better
Than folks like us have any business with.
Farmers around twice as well off as we
Haven't as good. They don't go with the farm.
One thing you can't help liking about John,
He's fond of nice things—too fond, some would say.
But Estelle don't complain: she's like him there.
She wants our hens to be the best there are.
You never saw this room before a show,
Full of lank, shivery, half-drowned birds
In separate coops, having their plumage done.
The smell of the wet feathers in the heat!
You spoke of John's not being safe to stay with.
You don't know what a gentle lot we are:
We wouldn't hurt a hen! You ought to see us
Moving a flock of hens from place to place.
We're not allowed to take them upside down,
All we can hold together by the legs.
Two at a time's the rule, one on each arm,
No matter how far and how many times
We have to go."

                    "You mean that's John's idea."

"And we live up to it; or I don't know
What childishness he wouldn't give way to.
He manages to keep the upper hand
On his own farm. He's boss. But as to hens:
We fence our flowers in and the hens range.
Nothing's too good for them. We say it pays.
John likes to tell the offers he has had,
Twenty for this cock, twenty-five for that.
He never takes the money. If they're worth
That much to sell, they're worth as much to keep.
Bless you, it's all expense, though. Reach me down
The little tin box on the cupboard shelf,

The upper shelf, the tin box. That's the one.
I'll show you. Here you are."
                              "What's this?"
                                      "A bill—
For fifty dollars for one Langshan cock—
Receipted. And the cock is in the yard."
"Not in a glass case, then?"
                              "He'd need a tall one:
He can eat off a barrel from the ground.
He's been in a glass case, as you may say,
The Crystal Palace, London. He's imported.
John bought him, and we paid the bill with beads—
Wampum, I call it. Mind, we don't complain.
But you see, don't you, we take care of him."

This passage from "The Housekeeper" may be taken
as one of Frost's tributes to John Hall and to the preoccupations of the poultry fancier generally (and one
interested in poultry, and at various periods an active
poultry raiser, Frost himself continued to be throughout
his life). But perhaps the purest poetic tribute he paid to
his own—as well as by poetic merger to John Hall's—
hen-breeding labors and hopes is found in the tender
and touching piece entitled "A Blue Ribbon at Amesbury." Shortly after that poem appeared in *The Atlantic
Monthly* for April, 1936, a fellow-poet asked Frost how
he had happened to write on so peculiar a subject. Never
pleased with such questions, Frost bridled resentfully:
"You don't like it?"
"Well, it's not one of my favorites," replied the other
poet, cautiously. "But I like it all right."
"You've got to like it *a lot*," Frost warned, "if you want
to stand in well with me."

26

Thus the conversation ended. But enough had been said to imply that "A Blue Ribbon at Amesbury" occupied a special place in Frost's private scale of values. One can easily guess at the reasons. It may have been partly because the poem epitomized for him those wistful years of his own poultry farming in Derry, partly because he caught therein all the dreams of what might have happened to his own birds (and never did happen) at poultry shows in Amesbury or elsewhere, and partly because Amesbury and all those dreams were associated for him with his real friend John Hall.

There is another important tie between "A Blue Ribbon at Amesbury" and another friend of those Derry days. Long after Charlemagne Bricault had given up the poultry business and had moved from Andover to Haverhill, Massachusetts (where he practiced as a veterinarian, served for many years as city Milk Inspector, and won recognition, also, as a breeder, not of chickens, but of Boston terriers) and long after Robert Frost had established a national and international reputation for himself as a poet, the paths of these two men seem to have crossed again. Nothing is known of how often they may have met in these later years, of how or where their meetings may have taken place, or of what they talked about together. Circumstantial evidence for one such possible meeting is contained, however, on the flyleaf of a particular copy of Frost's book *A Further Range* (1936). There, in the author's hand, inscribed "For Charlemagne Bricault," are the last six stanzas of "A Blue Ribbon at Amesbury." The heading used for the extract is a single line taken from an earlier stanza of the same poem—a line which makes reference to the artist Franklane L.

Sewell, whose handsome illustrations of fowl had frequently appeared in *Farm-Poultry* during the period when Frost had been a contributor (and also during the period when Doctor Bricault had regularly advertised therein his White Wyandottes, "bred to lay"):

One a Sewell Might Have Painted

Tis ritual with her to lay
The full six days then rest a day,
At which rate barring broodiness
She well may score an egg-success.

The gatherer can always tell
Her well-turned egg's brown sturdy shell
As safe a vehicle of seed
As is vouchsafed to feathered breed.

No human spectre at the feast
Can scant or hurry her the least.
She takes her time to take her fill.
She whets a sleepy sated bill.

She gropes across the pen alone
To peck herself a precious stone.
She waters at the patent fount.
And so to roost, the last to mount.

The roost is her extent of flight.
Yet once she rises to the height
She shoulders with a wing so strong
She makes the whole flock move along.

The night is setting in to blow
It scours the window-pane with snow;
But barely gets from them or her
For comment a complacent chirr.

                              Robert Frost

Charlemagne Bricault may not have cared much for poetry. But those lines, inscribed for him by his friend and former customer, must have appealed to his own detailed knowledge of prize birds and must have invoked vivid memories. The lines may also serve to heighten any reader's awareness that Robert Frost's years as a farm-poultryman left their indelible mark on his literary career, as a prose-writer and as a poet.

E. C. L. & L. T.

Hanover, New Hampshire
August, 1963

Trap Nests

AIKEN had worn the starched collar of servitude to dress long enough; he wished to get back to loose clothes and the country, and he saw in hens a way.

He remembered the hens at home in his boyhood as more or less of a nuisance. They had roosted on the rolling stock and scratched behind the live stock in the barn, and what eggs they laid they were careful to conceal where no one could find them until rotten. But from all accounts they had become a different thing. There was easy wealth in them for whoso had the tip.

Aiken did not forsake all to go into the hen business, as many have done to their cost. He sat a high stool in the office of Somebody & Co., where the wages were small and the perils to life and limb, dyspepsia and writer's cramp, seemed numerous. But, although he did not like the job, it was his whole-wheat bread and butter, and he was too cautious a man to abandon it for an uncertainty. So he made a preliminary experiment in the hen business on a very small scale in his back yard, through the instrumentality of his wife.

He provided Mrs. Aiken with all the literature on

hens that he could come at, and told her to go ahead. Only he expected her to make it pay. He had heard of three dollars a year in a hen, and he asked her to bear that in mind.

Mrs. Aiken was a practical little woman with an English accent, and as it was to save Aiken from a sedentary life or die herself of married life, she went at the new business with a will. At first she seldom troubled Aiken with her doubts and perplexities. She faced alone the problem of fixing on the only right breed of hen for beauty and use. Unassisted she attacked the large subject of feeding for eggs.

First she fed cut clover for a while exclusively, then green cut bone exclusively, and finally, in despair, a balanced ration prescribed by an irresponsible editor. But she fed without results. It is true that the hens did not die; the adult hen is hard to kill except with a weapon. But they did not lay and Mrs. Aiken was at her wit's end.

Once more she tried steamed cut clover, which she had the greatest faith in for its aromatic odor. Then, because she had to, she appealed to Aiken. He had heard that the chief reliance of the new poultryman was green cut bone. But she had fed that, morning, noon, and night, for a week, and it had come nearer sickening the hens than anything else. Aiken told her what she already knew, that he did not wish to be bothered. He told her to feed anything she pleased— all he cared about was results.

Mrs. Aiken had been thinking. She could not say

that all she cared about was results, but she cared a
great deal for results. She would have been glad to
consider her hens too, but if they would not let her,
was it her fault? Though of a kind heart, she was no
sentimentalist to prefer suffering herself to seeing
dumb beasts suffer (and when you come to think of
it, hens aren't but a dumb little dumber than they are
beasts). If the hens wouldn't lay, they should be made
to lay—she would have recourse to the barbarous trap
nest—they had brought it on themselves—she washed
her hands of the responsibility.

She had held trap nests in reserve for some time.
She brought herself to mention them to her husband.
He had heard of them. He entertained some such idea
of them as she, namely, that they were intended to
catch and hold the hen until she was willing to purchase freedom at the price of an egg—hold her to
ransom, so to speak. He would have had no scruple
in employing them himself, but for a woman it was
different. They really did savor of vivisection and the
Inquisition. Mention of them gave him pause.

"Heroic measures?" he said with an attempt at
lightness.

"I hate to do it that bad," she said.

"And I won't let you do it," he spoke up like a man.
"I'll do it myself. Someone has got to suffer, and I
guess it'll be the hens. Buy the nests."

"We can make them," she said. "They are like or-
dinary nests, except that they have doors like a boot-
jack hanging on hinges from the top, the points of the

inverted 'V' resting on the inside of a sill so that it can only open inward."

"Very well, we will make them, and then none of the old maids in the neighborhood will be any the wiser."

So the trap nests were installed. The hens took the opposite side of the pen and craned at them with a scandalized cackling, and then forgot them, and went about their business—which was not laying. At that time they were on a diet of quartz and charcoal. They did everything that real hens do, and their little ways interested Mrs. Aiken the livelong day. They scratched, they preened, they went to roost. But they never laid, and, as barren hens, naturally avoided nests, and how much more these suspicious looking nests with closed doors.

Every night Aiken said, "Caught anything?" and Mrs. Aiken shook her head disconsolately. Aiken wasn't sorry he had kept his place with Somebody & Co. until he had investigated the hen business for himself.

"Say," he said hopefully one evening before he had cast his overcoat, "we forgot to bait those traps."

"There," cried Mrs. Aiken. "But what shall we bait them with?"

"What are you feeding them now?"

"Grit, principally," she said.

"Do they take to it?"

"They did at first, but I'm afraid they're what is called 'off their feed' again. I might try cheese."

"No, starve them a day or two and then try corn."

The plan succeeded, and one night Mrs. Aiken had

to announce that all the hens were in custody and most of them in one nest.

"Probably the first hen in acted as a decoy, and the others followed till there was no more room," he surmised. "Well, they'll keep each other warm."

"They are gasping now from the heat."

"That's but one inducement the more to make them do as they are asked. They'll know what it is to serve on a jury."

"But if one of them should lay an egg, how shall we know which one it is to release her?"

"The good will have to suffer with the bad—the Lord will know his own, as the bishop said." Aiken took a growing satisfaction in ruthlessness, for such, he felt, was life.

But the hens were obdurate. A week passed and there was not one egg. Aiken began to reconcile himself to the thought of lifelong bookkeeping. He saw nothing for it but to acquire the use of his left hand in writing.

"I know they can if they will," he told his wife irritably.

"But perhaps they can't will. It seems to me they're too nervous to concentrate on laying or anything else."

"I wonder who invented trap nests, anyway. Did you ever hear of their profiting anyone?"

"I know they're used. But they seem so cruel. Still, they're no worse than stomach-pumps to feed hens with."

"Do they use those?"

"Yes, it's called intensive poultry keeping."

"Intensive, huh! Well, I'm going to let the farrow song-birds loose, and we'll get out of the business faster than we came in."

So said, so done. The doors were opened and the hens staggered forth on their hocks—those that were left. Several lay trampled flat as a pancake. One of the survivors burst into a meaningless cackle. It was the persistence as well as the quality of the noise that infuriated. If she had been satisfied with a stanza or two in that vein, Aiken might have borne it. But she was a hen, and Aiken was human and a dyspeptic. He kicked that hen through a window and drove the others through the door. Then he shooed them all to the top of the yard fence, where they sang together like the stars at the creation—thence broadcast over the neighborhood.

"How unreasonable," said his wife. "You can't get out of the hen business as easy as that. Your chickens will come home to roost."

"Will they? I'll stay here and see that they don't."

And armed with a broomstick, he stayed.

A Just Judge

T HERE was once a ninety-six point hen, and she was a ninety-six point hen, and she really existed, and this story recounts only facts. The judge that first scored her said to the man beside him who footed up the cuts, "Well, that is the least I can give her." He might have been pardoned for saying, "Well, that is the most I can give her," but that was not that judge's style.

She was what is called a chance bird. Not that she did not come of good stock. Her parentage was not altogether obscure. Only there was nothing in her ancestry that quite accounted for her, and she outclassed all her sisters and her cousins and her aunts, some of whom were on exhibition with her at her first show.

That judge said privately that he would have been glad to score her a hundred, and it seemed foolish not to, but he had to think of himself. "I made that score card in the sweat of my brow," he was reported as saying.

"Well, what were her defects?" some one asked him.

"You will have to consult the score card; I don't pretend to remember; the impression she left on me was one of perfection." Which was the making of that pullet.

From the time they hung the blue ribbon on her coop, she always had an audience to the end of the show. She was well trained and took it all as a matter of course. She showed herself front, three-quarters, profile, back, almost as regularly as a revolving show case. But she listened to the praise on every hand with composure, the more so as much of it would have made her of another breed entirely.

This story is about the confirmation of the first judge's judgment by that of judges that came after him. For No. 1 so to call her did not go home to the breeding pens of the man that raised her. She was bought, as it proved, for showing until used up, and sent on her travels. She had a cold winter. She made her debut early in the season, when the important shows were all to come. She went to them all by express in a draughty shipping coop, and at all of them she won first place, always with special mention from her judges.

But if she was worth anything as a breeder or to keep this was not the kind of treatment she was entitled to, and if she liked it herself at first, she soon tired of it. It ceased to console her that she was making one man's reputation. She became a bird acquainted with depot platforms in all sorts of weather. She learned to judge humanity at large by the treat-

ment she had received at the hands of expressmen. She suffered a disillusionment that manifested itself in a change in the carriage of her tail.

That was the beginning of the end. Next it was her face paled; then her legs lost their color; her eyes dimmed. And just in time to save herself from being ridiculed as a bird greatly over-estimated at the lesser shows, on the eve of the greatest show of all she collapsed entirely. She lay in her pen a heap of ruffled feathers, such a sorry spectacle as invited only pity. She had made a glorious campaign and this was the upshot. It would have been kinder to her reputation to have spared her a little and given her a chance to win at the only show really worth while.

But though she was plainly marked for death, she was not forgotten in her last hours. Experts told her story again over her prostrate form. She had more victories to her credit than any other bird of the season, and what a pity that she should not have been allowed to put the finishing touch to her record by winning here. She must have won, some said. It was doubted and argued. Judges present who had known and scored her were appealed to. With them it was a personal matter. They defended her with spirit. One said, "I firmly believe that pullet was sent into this world especially for this show—and look at her. It's a shame!"

A life-sized photograph of her was produced from somewhere, taken when at her best by a committee of some club appointed to revise the standard. Someone had written under it, "Real Perfection as distinguished from Ideal Perfection."

All this was vindication enough and more than enough for the opinion of the judge that had brought her out of the obscurity of her first show. But the remarkable part was to follow.

It was not generally known that even at the point of death the famous No. 1 found a buyer. In the excitement of the close of the show she was not thought of. By those that knew of her sale it was assumed that she was destined for stuffing and mounting. No one ever expected to see her again or hear of her either, after the echoes of her first season's achievements had died away.

But that was not the kind of pullet she was. She was bought at a risk by a man that knew his business and intended to give her a fighting chance—which was all she asked. She was carried far, far from shows and the fear of shows, to a settled life and natural conditions. And she amply repaid everything that was done for her, and came straight back to life, and before spring was well advanced was laying precious eggs, though considering her antecedents, they were probably not nearly as precious as herself.

She was lost to the world in the mountains of northern Vermont, where hens being known by the amount of noise and dirt they make, are not distinguished one from another. Her owner was of the quiet kind that prefer to let their belongings as well as their actions speak for themselves. She was not advertised and she had no visitors. She bucked the trap nest at least thrice a week, and as her eggs proved fertile in spite of what she had been through, by the end of the summer a good proportion of the chickens about the place bore the toe marks that related them to her. She tended strictly to business and her work showed that she had two at least of the requisites of a good breeder, she was prolific and fertile. Whether it would turn out that she could transmit her superior qualities was another matter.

But it was not merely as a breeder that her owner valued her. He had built somewhat on his hope of winning with her another year; but he did not underestimate the chances he took when he bought her with this in view. The chances were there: first and foremost, she might never recover; then if she recovered, she might never recover her original form; and there was always the chance that like many another wonder, she might not be able to hold her own through the breeding season and the moult. She soon disappointed his fears as to her recovery and her recovery of form, and with the care she had, she approached the moult with everything in her favor.

The moult is a trying time to the poultryman. He would gladly cut it out. There is not an object in sight to keep his courage up. The hens are a disgrace, and as for the growing stock, for all that one can tell, they may be all culls. It will be Christmas, it seems, before the youngsters throw the red or the oldsters reclothe themselves against the cold. One poultryman who always displayed the sign "No Admittance" on his houses during the last moult, in a moment of exasperation went and superadded the word "Positively" with his own hand.

No. 1 was as disheartening as the rest of them in the doldrums. She went to pieces all in one day like a smitten thistle head. She was as ready for a swim as anyone could be without the inclination, and she didn't seem to care how long she stayed so or who saw her. At length she began to grow short quills as if in her second year she intended to be a porcupine, but she took her own time about this even. "Better a porcupine," her owner said, "than that sort of an undrawn carcass." But finally his patience (what there was of it) was rewarded, and No. 1 was in feathers again.

And he swore that she was the same old bird. It often happens that fowl are so changed by the moult that their owners do not know them, nor they their owners. But No. 1 was the identical bird, or his eyes deceived him. Of course he might be partial—and then again he mightn't be. At any rate he was ready to back her.

The shows began. Poor No. 1, if she had known what was in store for her, would perhaps have contrived not to clothe her nakedness. She found out when it was too late that she was in for another strenuous winter. She made her first appearance near home; it was a small show but it was bad enough. The babel of roosters in the large hall, the smell of cats, and the uniformity of the coops made her deathly sick.

It was like reopening an old wound. She was expected to win there hands down, and she did, and this was the manner of it.

It was scoring time, and a group halted before her coop, among them her owner: but the one she noticed particularly, or should have noticed, since if she had but known it, she owed him a grudge, was the judge who had discovered her in the first place. There he was again with the same hypercritical look in his eyes or eyebrows. He began an inventory of her faults carelessly enough, but as he proceeded his expression changed. Suddenly he looked up and around him as if for an explanation in the faces of his audience. Finding none, he resumed his task, but with more and more perplexity.

"What do you make it?" he said at last.

"Four," said his attendant.

He took the card and regarded it with open mouth. "I wonder," he said. Then he crumpled it and thrust it into his pocket. "Try again! I must be getting old that I cannot find faults as I used to. Two in two years."

The result was the same. "Gentlemen," he said to the company, "who owns this bird and where is he? Unless I am greatly mistaken, she and I have met before. I scored a bird 96 points once and I never intended to score another that, if I could help it, and I don't believe I have, for I think she's the same one. Does anyone know if her owner is in the hall?"

"Here," said the individual in question.

"Do you happen to have any of the score cards this fowl made last year?"

"All of them, I think," was the answer. "Right here in my pocket. I bought them with the bird."

"Well, the first one has my name on it and I should like to see, and have the rest of you see, how it compares with the one I have just signed. She is the only bird I ever scored ninety-six."

The cards were held side by side. The judge beamed. "I said once that I should be glad to score her 100, because I wasn't sure I saw the faults I gave her, but I have found the same ones again, so they must be there, but, by cracky, they were hard to find —they were hard to find."

With the rest of her story we are not concerned. She was mercifully preserved from a repetition of her experience of the previous winter by the interference of the judge to secure her for himself. He bought her at a fabulous price, and kept her as a living witness to his own consistency as a judge.

A Start in the Fancy

THE man with the courage of his convictions was home from the Score Card Poultry Show with a ten-dollar pullet, and the fact got into the local papers and his neighbors dropped in to condole with him.

"Can you see that much money in a hen?" said one.

"Wasn't it this way?" said another, "the man you bought her of bought another of you for the same price, you both got the advertising, and not a dollar changed hands."

A third offered the man twenty cents a pound for her live weight. "It's easy to see she's an extra good hen," he admitted.

At first the man gloried in his shame. "Why, Mister," he replied to this, "that hen is worth more than your horse." But constant dropping wears away a stone, and bye and bye his neighbors' comment began to have its effect. He grew sensitive. The pullet was not his only folly. There was a cockerel also, which he had put off declaring, until now he was resolved not to declare it at all.

But if his neighbors would only have let him alone, he would have done very well. He was far from sick of

45

his bargain. He remembered with satisfaction the re-
luctance of the birds' former owner to part with them.
"Why, those birds," he said, "represent ten years of
breeding—ten years of my life, brother. Don't ask
me for them. To sell them at any price would be no
more ruinous than to give them away. They're not for
sale. Say I let them go—I should have to begin all over
again at the beginning. What should I say for myself
when I got home?"

And then he had always the score cards to peruse,
even more reassuring to the novice than the sight of
the birds themselves. One of them gave the pullet a
score of 95½, only one half point less than the limit
for females, he understood. Neighbors might say what
they pleased, but no amount of ungenerous detraction
could take that from him. The birds might go off their
feed and die, he still had the score cards to show for
his money.

He had taken the precaution to ask their former
owner if he considered them a well assorted pair for
breeding, for it sometimes happens that the best birds
in the world are obviously not mates.

"I should mate them," he had said, conservatively.

"Then I ought to get something good out of them
next year?"

"You ought—you ought," with the same cautious
reserve.

That was enough to build on. He felt almost certain
of justification in the offspring of his purchases, in the
show room of the next season. If others could sell pul-

lets for ten dollars, and cockerels for — well, for considerably more, what was to prevent his doing so? Such prices were common, he believed. They were in the very air of the show room. Scrub birds at scrub prices for scrub buyers, was the cry there, and the imagination of the man had been kindled.

But his neighbors wouldn't let him alone. They came every day, ostensibly to form their judgment of fancy poultry on the high priced pullet, but in reality to take a good look at the man that bought her.

Gentlemen came every day, not so much "to see what my good hen did lay," as to quiz the man with the courage of his convictions, though they asked about the laying, too.

"I suppose she lays," said one reflectively, "just like any other hen, for all she cost, — say, heard you gave ten dollars for her, is that right?"

"Yes, she lays," said the man evasively.

"Two a day?" And then the visitor launched forth into tales of hens that had laid two eggs in a day, and how the fact was known.

They came in doors on Sunday, and did their best to make the man unhappy. Their winks did not escape him. What the man did not realize was that they were in part inspired by jealousy.

They particularly resented his score cards — just as if, they said, the town had never had a scored fowl before. They plagued him with tales of 98 point hens here, there and everywhere. In vain he argued with them that a 98 point bird was impossible. He appealed to editors, but what could they help him in a community that recognized no authority but its own in its own affairs. He was taken to see 98 point hens with his own eyes. He hooted. He wanted to know who scored them. What judge had the courage to sign their cards! It was to no purpose.

The proud possessor of a 98 point hen came with a backing of scoffers, and made the man an offer. "I'll sell her to you," he said, "for five dollars, and you can call it you've *made* five."

"Why don't you let him have it for ten, just for the name of it, and give him a rebate ticket for five?" some one put in.

"How much would you let any one else have her for?" another said.

"Well"—the wag paused for the effect they had all come for—"well, what I could get, I suppose, so much a pound, live weight."

The man felt his courage going. At this stage he was not quite sure whether he was sorriest for having paid ten dollars for a hen, or for having been found out. He might have regretted neither, had he been less alone in the community. But he lacked moral support altogether. At least so far as he knew he had not won so much as a boy to his way of thinking. He had accomplished nothing and had suffered much. He thought he was right, that is, he hoped he was right, that is,—well, perhaps it would have been better to leave it to others to find out. Martyrdom to an idea was more than as a man with a family he felt equal to.

Still, he was not ready to acknowledge himself beaten. He kept up the fight, but it was with half a heart. In some vague way he looked for vindication in the future. The pullet's every egg was saved for incubation. Chickens came and for awhile they looked their prize blood. Then for awhile they didn't, particularly those consigned to a brooder which left too much to the inexperienced man. Not that all these died as might easily have been the case; only their feathering was eccentric. One was completely feathered at four weeks like a little bird with full-grown trailing wings. Another had ridiculous pantalettes. Another ran mother naked like a little boat on legs. At this point the man's courage was at the lowest ebb.

But if he had given up he would have lived to regret it. For it was not two years after that the same neighbors who had come out of their way to make sport of the first up-to-date poultryman in their midst were turning up-to-date poultrymen themselves. Excitement over the new poultryculture struck the town with a rush. Everyone talked hens and built paper covered houses. There was talk of a local show. Perhaps all this must have come anyway. Perhaps the man's sacrifice made it come more easily. Perhaps his example had been worth something. He would have had that consolation, but the chances are he would not have thought of it. He would have been a man with a grievance—against himself. He could never have forgiven himself for not hanging on.

And yet he surely would not have hung on but for

the merest accident. It happened one day in the fall when he had given up all thought, and almost all care of his fancy stock, that a business-looking man pulled up a spirited horse in the road before the house. His mouth had a muscular grip on an unlighted cigar, and he nodded unceremoniously, without speaking. What seemed to have caught his eye were the white chickens, now almost full grown that ranged the young orchard.

"What you got there?" he said at last.

"Rocks—White Rocks," was the reply.

"Yes, I see, but—"

"Oh, they're good ones," said the owner, with assumed confidence.

The visitor looked at his horse irresolutely. "Just hold this mare," he said authoritatively, and got down. "Or no—can't I hitch her somewhere? I want you to call your chickens up where I can get a look at them."

The horse was hitched, the chickens were called. The visitor walked around them with a scowl.

"Some farm-raised cockerels are just what I'm after," he said. "You've got two or three very fair birds there. How much will you take for say three of them and let me choose?"

"I ought to get five dollars, hadn't I?" said the man in an agony of doubt.

"For the lot?"

"No, apiece," said the man, weakly.

The visitor said, "Humph." There was silence for

awhile. Then the visitor turned a quizzical look on the trembling man.

"How many birds have you ever sold for five dollars?" he said.

"Ask me how many I ever bought for five dollars," said the man.

Again there was silence. Then the visitor said, brushing his knees, "I guess you're new to the business. Just to encourage you I'm going to give you five apiece for five. You round them up and crate them now, and let me see you off to the station before I go."

The man nearly dropped down dead. He experienced a sudden return to the courage of his convictions. Before he had quite recovered from the shock, he found himself back from the station, poorer by the loss of five good cockerels, (which he now for the first time really appreciated) but richer by twenty-five dollars, and some new ideas. He was saved to the fancy.

The last thing the visitor had said as he handed him a card on leaving was, "Drop me a line if you care to part with any of those pullets. But keep the price within reason, I'm no millionaire."

If the neighbors only knew!

The Question of a Feather

How an Editor Got Out of the
Frying Pan into the Fire

THE editor sat at his desk. He had been writing about hens all day, and he hadn't heard a hen since he left home in the suburbs in the morning, and he was tired of it. Perhaps the nearest live hens were in the death coops of the Faneuil Hall market. It was a hot day, and he had opened the window for air, but had let in only street noise and the smell of a livery stable. He was at his letters, and his brain reeled at the steady recurrence of the roup letter and the lice letter, and he was on the verge of things unimaginable when there came a fresh clear call from the fields.

It was just another letter, but the quaintness of it: "You see many poultry places in a year," it ran, "but perhaps have not happened to see—we thought you might be interested to see—a place of which it could be truthfully said, as of ours, that it was the result of following your instructions to the letter. Sister Martha has read your paper ever since we began to keep hens, and gives you all the credit for what we have made of our Minorcas. You have been our only teacher, and we want you to be the judge whether it has been to our advantage. We learn that you pass near us every day on your way to and from the city. Would it be overmuch to ask that you turn aside sometime to visit us?"

Here was precisely what the editor had always feared—that someone would follow his instructions to the letter, and therefore it had been part of his instructions that they should do no such thing. Before everything he had advised the use of judgment in keeping hens. So that if sister Martha had followed his instructions to the letter, be it upon her own head. He was sorry about her Minorcas. He wondered what sister Martha had managed to make of them—Leghorns or only scrubs. Still, he did not feel that he was to blame, and if he was, what was sister Martha going to do about it?

He smiled at his fancies, and as he did so looked at the clock. "I doubt if 'tis as bad as that," he said, "but just to see how bad it is, or how amusing, why not knock off now, and look in on them this afternoon when I'm in need of the recreation? I never have seen a place of which it could be truthfully said that it was all my doing, and while I am not sure that I shall derive much pleasure from seeing one, I had much rather see it myself than have anyone else see it."

As he found his coat and hat, he tried to picture to himself sister Martha, the poultry woman, his constant reader. He thought he knew the type—"Old maid," he said, "and the one that wrote the letter, too. Innocent, credulous kind, or under the circumstances I shouldn't trust myself to their tender mercies in a

53

lonely suburb toward supper time. Now if it was a man that wanted to confront me with his failure to make money in hens—but why speculate when I shall soon know."

On the electric cars he referred to the letter again, once for the address, and once to refresh his memory of the contents. He considered himself as having one of the good times incident to his calling. He liked nothing better than visiting a poultry farm, and visiting this one had a spice of real adventure.

"So here we are," he said at last, referring once more to the letter in front of a little vine clad cottage. The surroundings were almost rural. In the near distance lingered a dark clump of tall timber; there were fields and gardens and orchards. But here and there you saw a house going up, and you heard the sound of boards unloading, and of nails driven home. The city streets were there, too, though it was plain that the house he sought had been there before the streets, for it was set down without reference to their direction, like some mirage through which you might expect to see the more substantial objects behind it.

He satisfied himself from the safe side of the fence before it was too late to retreat had he cared to, that everything about the place was as it should be. The fruit trees were thrifty; the hen houses were right, and the yards were right, and, unless he was mistaken, the hens in them approximated Minorcas—Black Minorcas.

He thought as it was near feeding time he might catch someone out of doors, in which case he would make an informal yard call, and get home to an early supper and long evening. And sure enough, as he stood irresolute who should click the latch of the hen house door but sister Martha herself, (as her looks told him), in her hand, for a subject of conversation, a pailful of eggs.

"And so these are the Minorcas?" he said. "They lay well. How many do you keep?" He had been within a thought of saying, "So this is sister Martha," but had fortunately suppressed that as perhaps too much for a beginning. "I'm the editor of *Hendom*," he made haste to add at the sight of the lady's consternation.

"Oh, oh, Mr. Fulton. Won't—well, sister Martha—won't you come into the—" she appeared from her movements to break off in doubt as between house and hen house. She decided for the former. "Sister Martha will want to see you first. Won't you come into the house?"

So there was some mistake, and this was not sister Martha. Well, if it was not it ought to be, and he did not cease to assert her claims to the name until presently in the house he was confronted by the superior claims of the other.

His visit made the ladies sit up very straight. In their embarrassment they let slip precious moments without a word. As much to help them as to make himself at home, the editor conceived and executed a pleasantry.

"To which of you after myself, always after myself,

am I to give most credit for the pailful of eggs I have just seen?" But while serving to compose nerves, it had rather a sobering effect than the reverse. It was the author of the letter that spoke, "Sister Martha wouldn't be able to do much, you know, and so the work out of doors falls to me; but she is the one that is interested in showing and such things."

The editor, of course, had not known, but now he guessed. Sister Martha was an invalid, and the extent of her share in the hen business was looking at the hens through the window. It was only a sisterly fiction that made her chief poultryman.

The editor was properly subdued by the intelligence. Only after a prolonged pause did he attempt to give a more cheerful turn to the conversation by venturing to suggest that the subject of showing had been mentioned.

"Yes," said the author of the letter, "we have not shown yet, but if we are prospered in our stock this year, we intended to go to Boston in the winter, and perhaps New York, and that reminds me—Martha, that feather; you are just in time, Mr. Fulton, to help us with that feather on the leg of, I think, our best pullet."

"Pull it?"

"Yes, pullet."

"Help you pull it, I mean."

"Tell us whether it is right to pull it," she answered, flushed and serious.

His call to see the hens had degenerated into a call

on sister Martha, which was more than he bargained for, and now he found himself confronted with a very nice question of ethics that up to this time in his life he had always managed to avoid. The question of pulling feathers was one to which he had always thrown his columns open for discussion—freely, but you could ask anyone if he had ever joined in the discussion. He was above suspecting that he had fallen into a trap set by his enemies, but he liked the situation none the better. Perhaps he was unreasonably shy of old maids disposed to follow his instructions to the letter.

He was thinking, thinking, and Martha, seeing his difficulty, came to his rescue. "Perhaps Mr. Fulton doesn't care to take it upon his conscience to decide for us in such a matter. It is too much to ask him."

The editor laughed uneasily at her penetration. "Oh, don't consider me," he said gallantly, "anything I can do to help you." But he was none the less inclined to temporize. "How comes a feather on the leg of a Minorca?" he asked.

"I know, and she from one of our best matings."

"Bring her in," said Martha.

The bird was brought, and sat cowering on the center table, unmistakably a picture pullet.

"Isn't it a shame?" sighed Helen.

"I am afraid it is the temptation that is the shame," said Martha. "We have had pullets before spoiled by a single defect, and have not felt as now. It is because the fault is so remediable. And people ought to face their own temptations, and not ask others to face them for them."

"But temptation implies wrong, and we only asked Mr. Fulton to tell us if it is wrong."

"We know it is wrong."

The editor was grateful to sister Martha for letting him out. "Really," he said, "I wish you wouldn't ask me to decide for you. But I shouldn't worry; 'tis a long time before the shows; the pullet may shed the feather."

"But if she doesn't?" said Helen, who was inconsolable.

"She may develop defects less remediable than a leg feather."

"Oh, but she won't," persisted Helen. "She is well along now, and you know how it is with the Mediterraneans."

He looked closer for the feather. He wondered if they would thank him for pulling it by stealth. What prevented him from pulling it, and so ending their perplexity, he did not know, unless it was the fear of lowering himself in the estimation of two very respectful ladies.

"Well," he said, "I don't see but that you will have to give up the idea of showing her."

The sisters were glum. His visit had done them no good. He was disappointed. He reached for the knob of the door.

"I must be going, and I haven't seen your place at all. Perhaps some other time."

But one thing and another prevented his repeating the visit. He often thought of the two, however, and once alluded to them indirectly in an article on "Women and Poultry." And at the Boston show he looked among the Minorcas for the outcome of their moral struggle. There was their pullet, disqualified. If those goody goodies hadn't compromised by frankly showing her with the offending feather intact. Who but two old maids would have thought of that way out of it?

Old Welch Goes to the Show

After Getting Ready—Good and Ready

OLD WELCH did not care about having his neighbors in when he was getting ready for the show, because, as he said, "The laity don't understand, and can't be expected to."

Still, he did not admit that there was anything to conceal. He used to say, "I guess 'tis fair enough to groom and tame the birds a little before showing." He scorned the defence that if he was bad others were worse. Others might be worse, he was not bad. He was an honest man.

His saying about grooming and taming the birds obtained wide currency. He was asked, when caught in the act, which he called going over the birds for black feathers,—grooming or taming. "Taming," he answered, with the suggestion of a wink.

Of course that made the uninitiated laugh. But as long as the gossip was confined to the neighborhood, Welch did not care, and he knew that as long as he showed that he did not care, it would go no further and do no harm.

There is something fascinating about the like of Welch that peculiarly fits them for corrupters of youth. Welch always had one or more boys around him; and the boys seemed never to tire of asking about the black feathers—whether they were a defect or not, and never to tire either of the old man's unvarying answer: "I calculate the judges would full rather not see any."

Welch loved to please the judges. One of their peculiarities was a passion for featherless legs, and Welch did what he could to see that they got them. There must have been a Brahma cross for blockiness somewhere back in his strain, for he often had legs as fringed as a cowboy's. But that was one of the easiest things remedied—according to the boys.

Old Welch's were White Wyandottes, and he was reported as saying that all he asked of nature was the Wyandotte, and he could supply the rest. "You just put a little of this here chloride of lime in the water on washing day, and—yes, it deadens the feathers, but a dead white is what you're after."

He revealed these trade secrets to the boys that sought him for their first taste of the fruit of the tree of the knowledge of good and evil. And the boys retailed them at the village store, where it was simply opined that Welch probably hated to win.

Welch usually had his chickens out early, and the showing season seldom found him unprepared. But one year his first hatches were so exceptionally fine that the gods fell in love with them, and they died young. His later ones were quite as good, but as they were too late to be of any use to him, he was allowed to keep them. Welch was eloquent in his racy way. His favorites among the boys sought his society every day, and he got all his dirty work done for nothing.

"What are you going to do about it?" one of them asked him.

"Do? I ain't got nothing to do with." For an artist like Mr. Welch this was a confession indeed.

"Can't you show yearlings?"

"This strain ain't bred for yearlings, sonny." By which he was understood to mean that his strain did not hold up well—were good for one year only.

"But can't you doctor yearlings?"

"Doctor, doctor. Don't use that word to me, son."

The boy was too old to be easily cowed, so he only said, "Well, groom and tame them, then."

This appealed to the sport in the old man, and he was mollified.

"Let's see how many we have got of that first lot," he said. "All I ask is maturity. They must have maturity. I can't furnish that. I suppose now a woman could —at least she could make them look younger than they are. But there's no use in my trying. I'm a man, and a plain one. I want 'em old enough, and surely that ain't asking much. I must get to the shows with something, or I shan't know 'tis winter, except by the cold."

"What's the matter with that fellow?" said the youngster, with something of the real air.

"Haven't I learned you no better than that? Why, there's pretty nearly everything the matter with him. His comb don't fit, his eyes ain't mates. He's yellow, and his legs ain't. He's too high posted. He's whale backed and hollow chested. But just to show you what I can do, I'm going to take that dog shaped specimen, and renovate him—renovate him."

"His eyes ain't mates, come to look at them. How will you fix that?"

"I've thought of a way. The hardest will be to make him throw a chest."

What follows rests on the authority of boys, and not particularly good boys. It received a partial confirmation from chance witnesses, and from the established fact that when the time came old Welch went to the show.

One day a visitor came upon Welch by the kitchen stove, with a cockerel between his knees, and a hot wire in his hand. "Taming that one?" was the ready question.

Welch was in a serious mood. "This is the way the pick of the comb is brought down to conformity with the head—by searing underneath." You would have thought it was the regular thing. The visitor's levity was rebuked.

Someone else was a witness to the finishing touches on the bird. Welch was polishing its legs, "just as you polish your shoes when you're out to be looked at," he explained. "That? Oh, that's butter color; brings out the yellow a little, maybe—but that's what the judges seem to like."

"Call it grooming or taming?" the other wanted to know.

Welch had heard this too often to resent it for anything but its age. "Speaking of taming," he answered patiently, "I never had a bird as tame as this one, especially on one side, where he's absolutely tame." He proved it by making sudden passes at the left eye, which never blinked. "He's tame on the other side, too, but not *as* tame."

There was only the boys' word for it, but it was believed that Welch had employed the services of an oculist in renovating the bird. One of the bird's eyes had been yellow; after the encounter with the oculist it was red like the other, but he did not seem to notice anything with it.

The boys said "glass." The boys said almost anything. They told about what might be called a pneumatic front. Welch had got the idea from the Asiatics who, he had read, practiced inflating the skin of camels with air to make them salable. It was a delicate operation, almost requiring the services of a veterinary. His instruments were a sharp knife, a bicycle pump, and needle and thread. Of course this was left to the last moment for fear of mortification.

Now everything was accounted for but the bird's general shape. Let what follows be spoken with reserve. You are not asked to believe it. The poor, the much enduring bird's lines were corrected, it was said, with a pair of Wyandotte shaped corsets designed by Welch, and made to order. You may say that you never heard of such a thing. You never did hear of such a thing, because no such thing ever existed until Welch devised it (if he did devise it). Therein lay his originality as a breeder. He literally recast that cockerel. It took two weeks of the tightest lacing known to fashion to satisfy the old man. Once or twice the lifelike glass eye was actually squeezed out in the process, and had to be searched for and put back. But in the end science triumphed.

Old Welch was a proud man when he surveyed the finished product. " 'Tis the best job I ever did," he said, "all things considered. What's the use of breeding in for a term of years, when you can make all the wonders you want practically out of mud, at trifling cost?"

"But," said one of the boys, doubtfully, "I should think a good deal would depend on the judge when you showed a bird like that."

"It does—it does. You have to be extra careful in choosing your judge. 'Tis with judges, as with other folks, there ain't only now and then one that's suited to your purpose. Now I only know one judge this year that that bird'll do to show to."

The old reprobate was so pleased with himself that he must take a boy to the show with him, and introduce him to the old timers as a natural born breeder.

The cockerel was Welch's only entry, and it had a red ribbon on its cage. The boy who told the story might as well have made it blue while he was about it, but he said red, and red we must keep it. Red was satisfactory to Welch.

Welch might easily have sold the bird, but when it

came to that his conscience smote him. He had a code of his own. If the right person had made him an offer he might not have been so virtuous, but he could not bring himself to palm his work off on a greenhorn, especially one that did not pretend to be anything else.

The greenhorn had picked up some of the technicalities, and he was particular to ask Welch, as a friend, if the bird was not a "chance bird."

"Chance bird," said Welch, with a twitch of the lips, "better say design. I designed him, made him out of whole cloth. I can talk this to you, because you won't understand. The fact is, he owes just the leastest leetle mite too much to the way he was groomed. I shouldn't want to recommend him to you, because I ain't quite sure that he'd breed true, and you may know that I wouldn't say so unless there was reason."

The Original and Only

"Y OU want to hear about our hen," said the practical poultryman, "the original and only — the hen that diverted us from the fancy, and laid the foundation for our present profitable egg business.

"Well, I bought her for her shape and color, and for nothing else, with no thought of the eggs in her — they might be solid gold for all I cared. She was a prize bird, but that wasn't what I bought her for. I bought her because she suited me. I had the mate to her, as cocky a cockerel as you ever saw, raised right on this place, and as I was going into the fancy for keeps, I paid twelve good dollars for that hen. It was a genuine plunge for a conservative farmer. I was five years younger than I am now, but I did just right. I'd do the same thing again today. She was a good beginning. She'd have been the making of us if we'd staid in the fancy, only she didn't let us stay.

"I remember well the day I got her home here. It was early in December, but cold as January. She was given the run of the barn for the time being, along with another bird I had picked up at the show, until I could make up the pen they were going into. The barn was no place for her in such weather, but she hadn't been there an hour when that boy of mine comes into the house and reports, 'That hen's laid another egg.'

" 'Which one,' says I.

" 'The one that laid in the box in the cars on the way—'tis the same egg.'

"I got to know that egg before long as well as my own name. It was a light glossy brown, flecked with pink. I can show you a specimen that we keep blown as a trophy.

"I said to myself, 'That's a pretty good hen not to let anything interfere with her plans like that. I wonder if it would stop her laying to pluck her.' I vow I don't believe it would, though come to think of it, I can't say that she ever laid in the molt, and that's about the same thing as being plucked by nature. But I never asked her to lay in the molt. She laid hard enough anyway to scare a man. I was always afraid she couldn't keep the pace, or something would go wrong, and finally it did. She got to making eggs faster than she could lay them. They came so fast that they crowded each other and broke, and she died of sort of an internal custard, so to speak. But I'm getting ahead.

"Along at first we didn't know which hen she was. I said to the boy, 'You make it a point to find out which hen is doing this.' He said he couldn't tell them apart. I told him to lift them off the nest and get the numbers on their leg bands. We didn't have any trap nests on the place then. The boy was our first trap nest. He deserves some of the credit for what followed.

"It turned out that No. 5 was the layer—the prize bird, the one that cost twelve dollars. I paid for her show points and got her eggs thrown in, but her eggs alone were worth the money. Not that she laid enough to bring that much in the market, though there's no telling what she might have done if she'd lived long enough; but they were worth it for what they taught me. For one thing, they taught me the importance of the egg of the best bred hen, which is something I doubt if one in a thousand thinks of in buying, and it wouldn't do one much good if he did think of it. It was the contrast between her egg and that of the other hen, I suppose, that brought it home to me. The other hen laid about once a week, and when she did lay it was a dead white, gritty, thin shelled egg, just mis-shapen enough at the pick to be unhatchable. She was money thrown away, though she wasn't bad looking.

"Of course at first all I saw in No. 5's eggs was fancy chickens. I was glad she laid good eggs, and laid often, because it meant chickens, and lots of them. But one day the boy said something that set me thinking. 'It seems to me,' he said, 'that that No. 5 lays three days and rests one.'

" 'Are you sure of that?' I said.

" 'No, I'm not sure.'

" 'Well, don't say anything you aren't sure of. Make sure. There's a calendar; you can keep score for her on that.'

"So a fire insurance calendar on the wall was our first egg record book.

"The boy was right; she did lay three days out of four; when the days got longer, four out of five. I said to myself: 'If there are other hens like that there must be others still altogether *unlike* that to pull down the average, because we think we're doing well at this season if we get half as many eggs as we have hens. It looks as if there must be some hens that only lay one day a week to offset the work of those that lay every day but one. 'Tis plain that a poultryman is as much in need of a weeder as a market gardener, and what's the trap nest but a weeder?'

"Suddenly I saw the trap nest in a new light. Before that it had been associated in my mind with big egg stories and line breeding for eggs. But it has no necessary connection with either. One needn't abuse his trap nests to make his hens too prolific for the stamina of the stock, if such a thing is possible; neither need he lie about their findings, neither need he tell the truth about them if the truth was so remarkable as to look like a lie. He could keep his mouth shut in that case. There may be such a thing as a 300-egg hen, but I'm not going to be the fellow to say so—not at this stage of the game. If you watch you'll see how careful I am not to be too definite about No. 5's laying. I am satisfied to claim for her about 200. It was more than that. But you don't catch me saying whether it was one more or a hundred more.

"I don't know whether I should have made a success of the fancy or not, and probably never shall know, because right at this point I was diverted from it for good and all. The trap nest as a weeder appealed to me as a sure thing. I felt that the fancy was considerably chancy. Fanciers are born, not made, and I wasn't sure that I felt particularly born, and as the ministers say that's the test, if you don't feel as if you are called you aren't called. There were already a lot of good men in the fancy who easily made the birds it would probably be cheaper for me to buy. And as far as I knew, the ranks of those who were tending strictly to the trap nests were mighty slim.

"You see what one hen can do. We knew that she laid 200 eggs—call it that. We didn't have to take anyone's word for it. It don't satisfy you, but it satisfied us. It gave us faith to go ahead. It gave us a sound basis to figure on, which is the hardest thing in this world to get. We have housed about 400 hens for years, and they laid for us upwards of 125 eggs a year; if they could be converted into 200-egg hens, by selection or otherwise, it would mean a clear gain of $1.50 per head with very little extra trouble. It would just double profits at what it costs us to feed, and what we get for eggs at wholesale.

"You may form some idea of what No. 5 may have been for shape and size and constitution from the general appearance of our flock today, for they are all her offspring in the fifth and sixth generations. They were not bred exclusively to lay. They were bred for everything that No. 5 was, and that was a good deal. But we are not afraid to say that we believe in eggs—we believe in the 200-egg hen. I am not prepared to say just how common she is, but probably not over-common. Two hundred eggs should be enough to entitle a hen to the name of the new hen, for of course we are not to have the new everything else without the new hen, and the new hen must distinguish herself from the old hen and the old pullet by marked superiority as a layer. She is not to crow or sport sickle feathers or talk politics. She must succeed without going out of her sphere.

"I'm going to observe the same caution about making claims for our 400 as I did for No. 5. We haven't got them all up to the 200 mark yet, not by any manner of means, and we've got some above it. It would surprise you to see the average—if you could believe it. They do very well—very. Of course 400 hens are not many. Now neighbor Davis over here is a real poultryman. He has something like a thousand in a three story building with no dirt on the floors except what the hens supply. We can't compare with him. But I sometimes think neighbor Davis isn't as fat as he used to be, and he talks too much of Belgian hares and squabs and ginseng for a man that's satisfied with hens."

Three Phases of the Poultry Industry:

A Typical "Bred to Lay" Business

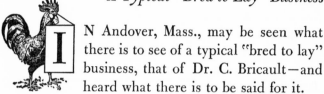I N Andover, Mass., may be seen what there is to see of a typical "bred to lay" business, that of Dr. C. Bricault—and heard what there is to be said for it.

Before going into what I saw at Dr. Bricault's place, I may state what I did not see. I saw 200-egg hens—or let us call them heavy layers—Dr. Bricault prefers that name—but no outward marks to distinguish them as such. We must take some things on trust in this world. Of course no one pretends to tell a 200-egg hen with the naked eye, or even with the help of the X-ray. A man may assert that he has exceptional layers, and we may believe that he has or not as we like. We may know whether he has or not, as we may know whether another man sells standard bred stock or not, by a small expenditure—the price of a sitting or two of eggs, say, or of a trio of birds. We generally have to pay to find out about the business that appeals to us from a distance through advertising.

What Dr. Bricault says about the part of his business that you must of necessity take his word for seems to me entitled to respect for its moderation. Perhaps as much as any breeder for eggs can claim is, (1st) that he has been at it long enough to have picked out a few good layers on which to build; (2d) that he has the apparatus to do with; (3d) that in so far as is practicable he is tending the trap nests. Dr. Bricault claims no more.

In the six years he has been breeding for eggs he has made a good beginning—that is all. He has come across some very heavy layers. This is not the place to discuss the existence of the 200-egg hen. Doubters may be referred to the recent bulletin of the Maine Experiment Station, which reports thirty-five 200-egg hens in a total of 1000 tested, or three in a hundred. Perhaps it will not be too much to ask the cautious to believe that Dr. Bricault has had and still has his 200-egg hens; that he has bred from them; that he has made something if not the most of them. It is early yet to speak of positive results in breeding for eggs; suffice it to say Dr. Bricault has achieved enough in that direction to encourage him to persevere.

It is interesting to know just how much Dr. Bricault pretends to devote himself to the trap nests. At this time of year all his nests are frankly and shamelessly fastened open. The record keeping ceased in July. He will base his opinion of the hens on their work for the nine months preceding. From November to July he was a slave to the trap nests—not absolutely, but more or less, and within reason. He made no bones of taking a day off occasionally. He is not a scientist, but a business man, and attempts only the practicable. His records then lay no claim to scientific accuracy, but are thought to serve the purpose if they discriminate roughly among the good, bad, and indifferent layers.

So much for Dr. Bricault's claims; now for what he thinks he can convince the most sceptical of by ocular demonstration. In entering upon his present work he has had to consider one important question: Can hens stand the strain of being bred to lay? He has answered this question in the affirmative, as he believes all must who having eyes will see. His growing stock are before you, some hundred and fifty pullets, practically all of them bred to lay. They have their family defects, as what breeder's have not, but no outward signs of weakness. Dr. Bricault will back them to rough it with the hardiest. Some are destined as an experiment to winter in piano boxes with free range on the snow, and he has no fear of the result.

One can see for himself moreover, though he must take the 200-egg hens on trust, that Dr. Bricault has the apparatus by which the 200-egg hens are brought to light—the notorious trap nests. He has the houses too for effective work, well planned, with every convenience, and manifestly well kept. His farm is of five acres, large for a village place, and his stock have the run of it—at this season both old and young together.

Let me say here that for his purpose no more ideal place than Dr. Bricault's could be found. One of the pleasantest spots in an unusually attractive town, it is calculated to add materially to the effectiveness of its white feathered population. It is high and dry without being arid. In fact every square foot of it would be available for almost any kind of farming. Not the least of its advantages is its convenience to the cars, leaving no one an excuse for condemning Dr. Bricault's stock or methods unseen.

Dr. Bricault has this to say about his position: "I do not insist too much on the 200-egg hens. Call them heavy layers. I took their measures when somewhat more enthusiastic than I have been this year or intend to be henceforth. Strictly speaking, I shall have no 200-egg hens this year. My best record is 160 eggs in a period of one year less three months. What the three months would have brought forth we shall not quarrel about. I am content to rest on what I am sure of. I do not wish and never did wish to be identified with the 200-egg interest. I wish to be known for what I am doing more than for what I possess. What if I have a few 200-egg hens? So have others. I am distinguished from most of these by what I am doing with my 200-egg hens. I am of those who believe that the 200-egg hens indicate an upward tendency that may be hastened by artificial selection; that they may be made to uplift all hendom in productiveness, and this without detriment to the stamina of the stock. I breed accordingly."

Whether we approve of Dr. Bricault's course or not, we must admit that he persists in it with his eyes wide open. He is familiar with the stock objections to his business. He divides them into two classes, the trivial and the general. The first make the trap nests their point of attack. The trap nests, it is said, worry the

hens out of condition, make them feverish and so
broody. The trap nests teach egg eating. The trap
nests do not catch the eggs. Those who use the trap
nests abuse them to pick out their poorest layers for
sale. The general objections resolve themselves into
two: that hens cannot be bred to lay more eggs, having already reached the limit; that they cannot safely
be bred to lay more eggs. All these Dr. Bricault has
heard and has answers for, or else he would not be
doing business at the old stand.

The Nichols' Place

BEFORE ever I saw the Nichols' place I had it from
one of the best known butchers in Lawrence that
the Nichols' fresh eggs always commanded a price of
their own in the markets a cent or two above anything else.

Eleven years ago Mr. Nichols was a carpenter in the
city; Mrs. Nichols a mill operative. They knew as
much about the poultry business as they had heard,
namely, that it was profitable. It seemed to offer the
best means of escape from city life, for which they had
no love. So they looked it up and went into it, like
plenty of others who have since gone out.

They had five hundred dollars between them. Part
of this went for a six acre place in a rather out of the

way part of southern New Hampshire near the town of No. Salem, the rest they invested in hens. To sustain life until they should begin to realize on their investment, Mrs. Nichols continued at her work in the mills, which she drove to and from nine miles over the road.

Mr. Nichols turned his trade to account to build his own houses — and very neat houses they are. As the first one was, so is the last one, for Mr. Nichols found little to improve on in his original plan. They are rather high and pitch roofed, divided by wire netting into ten foot sections, with a passage in the rear. If they have a fault it is the draftiness, which I should think inevitable where there are no board partitions to break the air currents set in motion by the animal heat on a cold night; but if they serve the purpose, criticism is a waste of breath.

The Nichols adopted intensive methods, the only ones thought of by the enterprising beginner of eleven years ago. They have brought their plant to a capacity of from four to five hundred head, but I doubt if today it exceeds the limits of a large sized village lot. The hen house runs are many of them not over fifty feet in length, and, of course, verdureless; the chicken yards, probably no larger accordingly, are in no better condition. The stock are fed green stuff by hand. In fact, they do nothing for themselves — everything is done for them; but there can be no question about its being done well. There is not a better "kept up" place, cleaner looking or smelling within marketing distance of Lawrence. It is the Nichols' boast that they have not missed cleaning the roost platforms six times since they started in business.

They chose the broiler and egg business, and eschewed the fancy. They make no pretense at breeding. They take the American hen as they find her, get her eggs, and at the end of two years "turn" her. Showing and shows they have little use for.

In raising broilers and getting eggs they have been equally successful. They have been able to name their own prices for eggs, not because they had better eggs than others, but a more constant supply. The butcher and grocer could pay what they asked when eggs were plenty, or go without when no one but the Nichols had them for sale. In October the Nichols are sending eggs to Lawrence at the rate of sixty dozen a week, and October is a worse month than December or January, market quotations to the contrary notwithstanding. As for their broilers, the fact that these were always passed along to the retailer by the commission merchant in the original package, unopened and uninspected, is sufficient testimony as to their quality.

I speak of the broilers in the past tense. The fact is, the broiler business languishes, and an explanation is due. It seems that for some time, if not from the first, the poultry business has been regarded as a means to an end. The end is cows, and the end is in sight. Having amassed the capital necessary to start with a good herd, they cast about for the time for their care. Something had to go, and it was the broilers, as the part of their work least to their liking.

So the Nichols have begun to enter into their reward; they have reached the point where they feel that they can afford to consult their tastes. The cows are the first thing; and they have begun to look around on their work and see how good it is. They take a natural pride in it. They have made a place literally bloom, that, judging from the original cost (inferred) could not have been much. They have increased it from six to over a hundred acres. They started with five hundred dollars; today their visible assets will foot up to four thousand, possibly more.

They have not done all this without setback. No one likes to be robbed of credit for his share of ill luck. Like others, the Nichols have had to learn by experience, but unlike some others they have hung on to tell the tale. Only this year they have known the greatest misfortune of all in an accident which befell Mr. Nichols, and threw all the work of caring for cows and hens on Mrs. Nichols. What can a woman do with hens, is a favorite theme with poultry writers; if they could meet Mrs. Nichols they would ask what can't a woman do with hens. She has run the place single handed, or practically so, having hired no more help than a man would hire in the same position.

But hard work has no terrors for the likes of Mr. and Mrs. Nichols. Whether from fear of being suspected of laziness or some other cause, they employ few labor saving devices in their establishment. There are no overhead tracks, no access for a wagon even to the pen windows. Sand is carried to and from the pens by the rear passage in coal hods. Everything is put through by main strength, but it is put through. And I surmise the fact is significant. The Nichols have succeeded, not because they started with ample capital, with previous knowledge of hens, with greater adaptation for it than for anything else they might have undertaken, or with special opportunities, but because they did not dislike hard up hill work.

A Typical Small Breeder

MR. JOHN A. HALL, of Atkinson, N. H., is a good type of the small breeder. He makes up in the care and real affection he lavishes on his stock for any lack of the business ability that distinguishes so many of our mere middlemen in the fancy. He is always heels over head in pets of one kind or another. In addition to White Wyandottes he indulges a taste for several varieties of ducks and geese, not to mention Runt pigeons and Angora cats on the side. All these creatures share the place of honor about the dooryard and everywhere under foot.

Mr. Hall has bred fancy fowl ever since he was "big enough to carry a dough dish." He has bred Rocks, Langshans, Cochins, Brahmas; and ribbons and trophies testify as to how he has bred them.

He has never faced the public as an advertiser. He might be regarded as a sort of breeders' breeder. That is to say, it is chiefly other breeders whose acquaintance he has made at the shows that find their way to him to buy. Still he says he has always been able to dispose of all the very good birds he could spare, and sometimes some that he could not spare.

But though he is a fancier first, he has never been so situated that he could afford to disregard the claims of the practical. He owns to having adopted the White Wyandotte for the most practical of reasons, to meet the requirements of his market for dressed poultry.

Mr. Hall has something like a hundred youngsters this year, all sired by one superannuated cock, and the family, though not over numerous, does the old bird credit. Not that they are all show birds, but there is a general freedom from disqualifications. There seems to be no feathered or willow legs. Eyes are good, plumage white to promising white. It is too early yet to judge of finer points of shape and style, but one thing is certain, the youngsters are all that they should be in weight, and that as White Wyandottes go in these parts is saying a great deal.

If houses are more to you than the inmates, you will go elsewhere than Mr. Hall's. The old timer will sometimes forget surroundings and accessories in the superior interest of the birds themselves. In the matter of housing Mr. Hall carries opposition to the sheltered life idea to an extreme. His houses have value to the observer only as illustrating what a hen will roost in and still live. They are airy to say the least. Mr. Hall apologizes for them, but I believe retains them on principle. He says the hens take no more harm from them than an occasional frozen wattle in winter, and on the whole are benefited by them.

Two things in breeding he makes of first importance —size and vigor. It is his experience that weight tends constantly to decline. It is a simple matter to keep it up, only it cannot be left to take care of itself. As for vigor, it is easier to get this right than not. What the stock need is a little judicious neglect. Mr. Hall's geese roost in the trees even in winter. Such a toughening process would be too drastic for hens, but these have to take it according to their strength.

As might be expected, Mr. Hall gives everything free range the year round. He fences in instead of out, finding that two and a half feet will keep hens out where it takes five to keep them in.

Almost any year you may see specimens of Mr. Hall's land or water fowl at some one of the shows, and as he lives rather out of the world, perhaps the easiest way to form an opinion of him as a breeder is there. It is worth a little trouble, however, to view his stock as a whole at home, especially his Wyandottes, because it is not everywhere in these days that you will see a lot as uniformly good.

The Cockerel Buying Habit

THE old gentleman took his corncob out of his mouth, and leaning toward me lowered his voice almost to a whisper: "What's your opinion of inbreeding, anyway?" he said.

"I'm a safe man to talk it over with," I laughed. "What's your opinion? There's no law against it, is there?"

"Law of nature," he suggested.

"I'd risk it."

"You're not afraid of it then?"

"Pshaw!"

He rolled his eyes on me with unfeigned admiration of my recklessness; but he shook his head.

"I snum I don't know," he reflected. "It's attended with awful consequences in the human family. You know how it's supposed to be when cousins marry. You can hear some awful stories against it."

"You can hear just as many the other way, and more authentic."

"Did ever I tell you how George Hill bred Cochins in till he got them that squat and fluffy and Cochiny they were a sight for sore eyes? But come to set their eggs one year there wasn't a single one fertile."

"I believe you have told me, but I don't think he proved anything. So many considerations enter into a case of the kind."

"Yes, of course it might have been something else. And maybe it's all prejudice on my part, but I snum I don't know. Don't seem as if anything'd ever make me feel about it as you do."

We had been on the point of considering his hens when the conversation took this serious turn. They were running at large, but as it was near feeding time a number had gathered around us as we talked. Our thoughts went back to them.

"Well, there they are, *such* as they are," said the old gentleman with a sweep of the hand. "It's as much as a year or two since you've seen them, I guess."

"What's the matter with those? They're a nice looking lot," I protested.

"If you don't see it, I'm not going to tell you."

All hens in a flock look pretty much alike at first glance, and it is hard to pick out individual characteristics. But I had to say something.

"Perhaps you mean they vary somewhat in size. You have some very white birds."

"I mean they're of all sorts and kinds. I've got some very white birds, and I've got some not so white. I've got some big ones, and I've got some all fired runts. The fact is they come every which way. I haven't anything like a strain."

As I looked I became convinced that there was something to what he said.

He sat down on his heels and pointed with his pipe stem. "There that one facing this way—tail to tail with that other one—she's eating now."

"Yes, I see her."

"Well, she's what I call a pretty middling fair bird —good full breast, and nice spread of tail. There may be a couple of others something like her in the flock— not exactly like—not on your life—but something like. I know where they come from. I know them as much as anything by a certain defect they all have—a hollow comb—worse in the males than in the females, of course—or more noticeable. They keep showing up since I bought a cockerel of So and so a few years back. Then take that one over there—alone—walking. She's likely to have a few stubs on her legs, though you can't see them from here. That's the tendency of the strain she comes from. But even if she hadn't feathered legs, and the other hadn't a bad comb, and both of them were all that they ought to be, they wouldn't be any more alike than the animals in a happy family at the circus."

I listened to this confession in silence.

As the old gentleman recovered his feet he shied a chip at another specimen. "And that one takes after What you may call 'im's strain. And there's another— I can tell you who breeds them like that—oh—now I know that as well as I know my own name—he lives out there in Milledge—never mind, it will come to me.

You see I've got them all and some besides, especially the some besides, the combinations that are neither this, that, nor the other, all right here together where I can study and compare them. But of course I could do that at the shows, couldn't I?"

"Not so much at your leisure," I consoled him.

"No, no, you're right there. I've had a chance to improve myself a lot. And no one can accuse me of having bred in. I could leave it to a jury of summer boarders if it looked as if I had bred in, couldn't I? And now what? At the age of sixty the indications are that I'm about ready to begin over again—dress the lot and begin over again. And I call myself a breeder? So much for the cockerel buying habit. And the question before the house is, another time shall I breed in?"

"Chance it—why don't you chance it?"

"That's what I asked you for—would you advise me to? I guess you don't think I could have come out any worse than I have, anyway."

"You don't think so yourself, do you? Come."

"Don't seem as if I could have, does it? But I snum I don't know."

"The Same Thing Over and Over"

ONE DAY an agent, who hated to take no for an answer, knocked at the door of Mr. Green with a poultry paper to sell. Mr. Green was at home.

Now Mr. Green is all right in his way. He has some nice hens, and he knows something about their care. Many in his place wouldn't shut them up so tightly, but then Mr. Green gets eggs, and eggs are what are wanted.

But Mr. Green confessed to the agent that he did not take a poultry paper—thought he didn't need one. He had taken one once, so that he knew what poultry papers were. He thought—and his wife agreed with him—that they were the same thing over and over.

"There's something to that," assented the agent with the best possible grace, "and I'm glad you spoke of it, because I know of nothing I'd rather talk about. There's necessarily a great deal of repetition in them."

"I was going to say it is all repetition," Mr. Green replied, "and between you and me, how much of it isn't? It was five or six years ago that I was taking a poultry paper, and I suppose they're still talking away just as they were then about cleanliness and warmth and a variety of feed. You see I have it all down pat."

"No, there has been a slight reaction from the high toned poultry keeping of those days, especially for those situated as you are, with many things to attend to besides your hens. It is allowable now for a farmer not to clean the droppings boards every day in the year. And as for warmth—warmth is not thought as much of as it was once. You may remember there was a time when people were putting steam pipes into their hen houses. I used to know a man that stacked his barn manure in compartments at either end of his hen house for heating purposes. The tendency would now seem to be all in the other direction—toward plenty of fresh air; it makes no difference how cold if only fresh. I spoke of your stoves just now when we looked over your houses. You say that you only use them on the very coldest days; but really they're the least bit out of date. And your double windows, too. The tendency now is toward no windows at all. If you haven't seen a poultry paper for five years, it is probably news to you that some are building hen houses, even as far north as this, with not even a wall on the southern side. The open front scratching shed is made to do duty night and day. So you see there has been some progress—or at least change."

"I guess not enough to pay a man to keep track of the poultry papers for five years."

"Perhaps that's a matter of personal opinion; but if the progress has been anything at all, I think the live poultryman would want to keep pace with it. It's the little things that make the difference between success and failure you know. You understand that I do not claim that there has been as much progress as you seem to think there ought to have been; and I will tell you why."

"Because you can't."

"No, not that exactly. To be sure I can't, but I wouldn't wish to. For just consider, what would you have, the whole poultry industry revolutionized, made over by the editor with each issue of his paper? That would keep things rather stirred up, and many complain that they are unsettled enough as it is with one advocating one method, another another."

"You're right there, all right."

"That's the way it seems sometimes, doesn't it, when one looks at details? But we'll have to admit that there's a surprising unanimity of opinion among experts on essentials, and that what are regarded as essentials, while not the same yesterday, today, and forever, change so slowly that they make some restless folks tired waiting—which brings us back to your quarrel with the poultry papers."

Mr. Green laughed at the agent's pertinacity as much as to say, "You're a good one, but you mustn't forget you're up against another as good."

"You may laugh," said the agent, "but I want you to see that this repetition in the poultry papers is a thing I'm not afraid to admit—is a thing, in fact, I count in their favor. Of course if their object was sensationalism it would be different. When poultry journalism catches the yellows from the other kinds of journalism, I suppose their object will be to reconstruct the poultry business twelve or twenty-four times a year, as the case may be. Meanwhile they are content to be merely progressive and up to date. In the principles they lay down they are much the same from year to year. Of course we are not speaking of the details of illustration and example — there they are varied enough for anyone. But in general principles they preserve a certain sameness, and necessarily so, because it is their function to reflect the poultry business, which changes no faster than any other business.

"I suspect that in calling them 'the same thing over and over,' you mean that they are not educational — at least for you — now that is that you have graduated from them. But even if you happen to be one of the few that know it all, they may still have their use in reminding you of things you know and are in danger of forgetting. And again, no matter how much they repeated themselves they would have a certain social value that must not be left out of account. Like intercourse with your fellow men, they are a luxury that amounts to a necessity.

"This is the way for you to look at it. Reading the poultry papers is precisely like talking hens with the most intelligent and enlightened, and where is the poultryman with soul so dead that he doesn't like to talk hens with almost anyone? It is not invariably educational, and one does not expect it to be, if he is an old hand; but it does stimulate and it does strengthen

91

one in his convictions. It affords one a sort of moral support in his faith in hens — a support that he may not need, and then again he may, if he is not quite self-sufficient and lives isolated, as most of us live in communities that have little use for hens."

That's the way the agent talked to Mr. Green. I don't recollect that he told me whether he got his subscription or not.

The Universal Chicken Feed

M R. CALL remained a seeker for truth to the end of his days in the hen business. (This is not an obituary. Mr. Call still lives, only not on the proceeds of his hens, or the expectation thereof.) In the fat months, when the hens laid, he staid at home and sawed wood, as the saying is; but in the lean months he went visiting. And because he was a pretty good sort of fellow, people always indulged his curiosity about their methods, and told him all they knew, especially with regard to feeding; but he never seemed to find out what he was after, for before long he was back again if possible more curious than ever.

"What are you feeding?" was his stock question, and though there was a discouraging sameness to the replies he got, he persevered with a devotion worthy of a loftier cause. He felt that there was something his hens lacked that once found would make them lay every day in the year. That something eluded him. Often he thought he had it. Once he grasped at sunflower seeds; he had heard of them before, but had clean forgotten them. Again, India wheat came to him as a revelation. He thought that an evening mash might be

93

better than a morning. He tried everything, only to be disappointed in the result. But because he had been many times disappointed was no proof that he was always to be. Hope sprung eternal in his breast. Sometime, somewhere, unless the public wearied of his quest before he did, he would light upon the right thing, and then begin to get his money back.

"I guess Call thinks there's some dark secret in feeding, or something that we're all keeping back," one neighbor remarked to another as they stood in the barn door one winter day. "He was over here to talk hens yesterday, and here he comes again now."

"Having trouble with his hens?"

"This is the time of year when he has trouble with them. How do, Silas? Hens started up any since yesterday?"

Silas was an honest man, and he realized that the first condition of getting help was frankly confessing your need of help. Who was going to tell him how to get eggs if he was getting eggs? No egg stories as big as a fish story for him. He was a little sour about it, but he owned right up. "Nary one. Where did you say you got those beef scraps you showed me yesterday, neighbor?"

"Those? I got those of Carey. But I don't suppose it makes so much difference where they came from, or who cut them up. Beef scraps are pretty much the same everywhere, though it seems as if one lot I bought did have a little more twine and skewers in it than usual."

Mr. Call went to a feed bin and examined critically the "article of scraps" it contained.

"How much'll you sell me a little of that for—a pound or two—enough to try it?"

"Give you some. But say, Call, I could tell you a way to make your hens lay."

"Why in the dickens don't you, then?"

"Because it's too simple; you wouldn't take any stock in it. You want to feed them something you nor nobody else ever heard of."

"Let's hear your way."

"Feed them a mash (as much as they'll hold of it in the evening) of scraps, corn meal, shorts, and middlings. Feed them wheat, cracked corn, oats, and barley in a litter. Keep shells, grit, charcoal, and water before them always. Give them plenty of green stuff. I use big cattle beets pegged onto a headless nail; it's surprising how they demolish them. And give them a dust bath, and give them air."

"I guess I must have done most of that."

"Well, you want to do all of it."

"Well, I guess I've done all of it; but I didn't get the eggs."

"Maybe you did some extras that spoiled it. Maybe you didn't do it long enough. There must have been something wrong. Perhaps your hens weren't females. But I knew how you'd take it."

Mr. Call went back to the feed bin and re-examined the beef scraps. What was there about those beef scraps?

Then neighbor No. 2 spoke up, and he was a wag.

"I'm not much of a poultryman, Mr. Call, but I manage to get eggs out of the few hens I keep."

"Table scraps?" beamed Mr. Call knowingly. "Yes, if we could only get enough table scraps to feed nothing else?"

"No; I have too many for that. You've never been over to my place. Better stop in some day when you're passing, and perhaps we can help each other."

"What are *you* feeding?"

"For one thing, protein."

This was a feeler. How much did Mr. Call know?

"Protein?" quoth Mr. Call. "Is that something new? Where did you get hold of it?"

"I take it you don't read the poultry papers, Mr. Call. Too busy, perhaps. Protein's something they recommend."

"It's a good thing, is it? Can you get it in town?" He turned to neighbor No. 1. "Have you ever tried it?"

"Yes, I have, Mr. Call," he reluctantly admitted.

"Why didn't you tell me about it?"

"Well, I guess I didn't think of it," said neighbor No. 1 rather lamely, and under restraint of fearful wink from neighbor No. 2.

Mr. Call's suspicions were aroused. Here was a strange omission on the part of a friend and adviser. He addressed himself to neighbor No. 2.

"Where did you say you got it — or don't you want to say? Is it a feed?"

"Yes, you'd call it a feed—not a medicine. Carey keeps it."

Carey kept it? Then of course they all used it. And he had been kept in the dark all this time. He felt aggrieved. How better could he show his displeasure with neighbor No. 1 than by ostentatiously thanking neighbor No. 2 for his information? He laid it on pretty thick, and neighbor No. 2 took it all with proper modesty, and saw him off for Carey's in quest of protein without a qualm of conscience.

But half way down the yard Mr. Call stopped. "Protein, protein," he had been saying. "Why drat my!" he exclaimed, "if it isn't in scraps. I've seen it in those analysises on bags—that's where. Seems to me it's in that last meat meal I tried." He half turned round, and then thought better of it.

"Smart, aren't they?" he said. "Well that's the last time, neighbor."

Dalkins' Little Indulgence

A Christmas Story

T IS no matter how much Dalkins paid for the bird; the point is that the man who sold it to him somehow got the impression that he did not pay enough— that he would have paid more. He could not have denied that Dalkins paid him all he asked. So that he had himself to blame if it was not enough. But he got to talking as if he had been cheated—and badly cheated. He enlarged upon the bird until he said he shouldn't wonder if Dalkins would get a cool fifty for it. He groomed it, so to speak, as he thought of it. He made it a little whiter than white, a little more symmetrical than symmetry.

As a matter of fact it was the kind of bird that is worth what one can get for it. It transcended scoring, as it was better than any score reputable judges are willing to sign. It was a bird framed by nature for comparison judging.

If the man who sold it to Dalkins made the mistake of parting with it for a cent less than fifty dollars, he deserved sympathy, but he was the only one who could see that Dalkins deserved blame. He showed himself a poor loser. He talked early and late to all comers about his misfortune that was another man's fault. But almost all comers had been in the same fix themselves, and knew how to make allowances. They did not believe too heartily in the pricelessness of his bird — a suspicion of which made him but talk the more.

The wonderful part of this story is that this fellow had picked the bird up away over back in Peacham, Vt., for one dollar and fifty cents. These figures I am willing to vouch for. In that case he did fairly well if he got a five for it. Mind you, I don't say what he got. At the time I heard various rumors. This part of the story must remain shrouded in mystery — men are such liars. I vouch for nothing that you cannot safely believe.

Though he was far enough away from this man and his troubles, the facts here stated somehow or other reached Dalkins. He had come by the bird through an agent of his who had spotted it by the merest accident from his carriage in passing. He had not been too curious about its history and antecedents at the outset; with him the bird in the hand was the thing. But a certain letter aroused his interest. It was anonymous, doubtless from someone in no way concerned, but bent on mischief making, and informed him that the remarkable bird had been raised by the writer's next door neighbor, and had been started on its career for one dollar and fifty cents. He questioned his agent about it. The agent had heard some such tale. Evidently gossip had been buzzing in the hill town of Peacham. He had heard also that the bird was of the

Dalkins strain direct. That was calculated to please Dalkins. He wondered if they couldn't find out who raised it. He would have liked the poor benighted fellow who would part with such a jewel for one fifty to know by its fruits what a thing the Dalkins strain was.

"He didn't suspect what he was doing," he said.

"It isn't likely," said the agent.

"And the fellow who sold him to you?"

"He had some idea, because he's kicking himself for having sold it. I have seen him since. He is talking at a great rate."

"The bird has made some stir already, then; that's what they call the fatal gift of beauty, isn't it?"

The agent was duly embarrassed. Dalkins was thinking.

"Say," he said at last, "I want you to find that original owner and bring him to the New York show on me. And bring the other fellow, too—both of them. I guess I'm good for it. Tell them 'tis a Christmas notion of mine—the show is near enough to Christmas for that. It'll make it easier for you. We'll show them a thing or two, and we'll show the kicker that he only knows a little bit more than the other fellow. And I think I'll show you something. Not a word of this to anyone outside, and not too many words to them. Just say 'tis my treat—consolation treat. 'Tis an order."

Dalkins' agent found the original owner away over in Peacham one bitter cold morning a day or two after Christmas. Peacham is a New England street town, that is to say, it consists of but one street, which runs north and south along a sharp ridge that looks like the back of a razor backed world. The railroad, when it was built, missed it by about eight miles on the right, and that seemed to send it into a decline —such a close call; no doubt. Many of its fine old houses are going to ruin, and there is never a new one to take their place. The age and size of its shade trees suggested that it might do very well in summer; but on such a day in winter it made the agent fairly groan at the patience of the people who could abide there. He inquired at the postoffice store for his man, and was sent to the woods for him. He came upon him snaking out logs in a grove recently laid waste, as seriously at work as if he had entirely given up seeing Santa Claus that year. He laid before him his invitation, and while not persuading him on the spot to accept it, succeeded in making him regard it as worth considering. At any rate, he carried him away in triumph from his toil like a Cincinnatus, a Putnam, or a Parker. He left his ox team standing in a brush pile in the care of his fellow workmen.

Before he left he had dinner with him, and it was all arranged. The fellow was a little sheepish at first, as one accused of deliberately circulating counterfeit money—only in this case it would have been a counterfeit bird. He suspected that his punishment was going to take the form of a practical joke. But he decided he was equal to it if only it wasn't to cost him anything, and the return ticket the agent laid down for him set at rest his fears on that score.

The agent had less trouble with the other fellow—Durgin, if the name must out. He considered the invitation his due. "Aw yes," he yawped, "he knew how it all was. Nobody probably intended to do him. It was business, just business. Only he thought," etc. Of course he wasn't a fool. He knew a good bird when he saw one. Only sometimes his mind didn't work quick enough, etc. Yes, he'd be glad to meet Mr. Dalkins. He bore no grudge. He wasn't that kind. Only he thought, etc. The main thing was that he accepted the ticket.

Scene, the New York show. Mr. Dalkins is doing the honors. When I say doing, I mean doing. He never let those two importations of his out of his sight for three days, and he never gave them a restful half hour. And it was not all inside the Garden. But let us draw a veil over anything that was irrelevant to the show proper. What have I to do with the Rialto and the Bowery? Suffice it to say that he gave two simple souls the time of their lives, and beat them out in his own enjoyment of it, in spite of the fact that it was on him and it came high.

The grand finale Mr. Dalkins had all prearranged, and he looked forward to it with the anticipation of a boy. No one had an inkling of what was coming, unless it was his agent to whom he once said in an aside: "The bird *the* bird, was sold, I suppose you didn't know, before anything was placed, but he's not to change hands till the last day of the show. I want you to be there when he does."

And once he had said to the second in line of possession, "So it sticks in your crop that you should have had fifty for your trade. Well, we won't let that spectre intrude on our festivities. Time enough for discussion afterward. There's always a way to settle such matters between gentlemen."

But the victim, though disliking the tone of banter in this, smelt not a rat. He and the original owner came to the final catastrophe as unprepared as the babe new born. They were so absorbed in the pleasure of the hour that it never occurred to either that he might be destined in the mind of the master to point a moral or adorn a tale. When it suited Dalkins' sense of dramatic fitness, they were led like lambs to the slaughter.

He towed the brace of them round to a certain much beribboned coop in the last hours of the show. He had made it a point to take them there several times a day during their stay to punctuate their experiences and keep them from forgetting to whom they were indebted for their popularity. He had never said much in the feathery presence. He found it more impressive to look in silence. His charges divided their hushed regard between him and the bird, awed by the thought of what great things might be passing in the mind of such a man at such a moment.

Now he led them there for the last time. Tomorrow it was good bye. The tumult and the crowing would die away. He told them that they must have a last look at the prize they had let slip through their fingers. Might it be a lesson to them!

As it happened they found someone there before them. He showed himself more than usually interested, and they hung back until he should have completed his scrutiny. Upon lifting his head from the note book he employed, he recognized Dalkins. He had been about to move off. He stood still. There may have been a momentary gleam of fun in his eye. It passed unnoticed.

"Splendid," he said, with an indicative wave of the hand, "I want him."

"I thought of you, Wilson, when I put him in here. Isn't he what you were looking for in the fall? I thought you would want him."

"I do. Your price?"

Dalkins made a movement with his fingers as if he despaired of having enough to give the sign. He ended by holding up, side by side, and far forward, one finger on each hand.

The agent, Durgin, and the original owner, turned pale. The first thought he was insane, the second that he was making a fake sale, the third that he hadn't been so far wrong in his estimate of the bird. To these three the two fingers meant two dollars.

"Shade it," said Mr. Wilson.

"Will you give me a dollar fifty?" laughed Dalkins.

"What are a few dollars here or there when it is a question of such a bird?" said Wilson as he went down for his wad.

"This is the payee." Dalkins obtruded the original owner.

"His bird, is it?"

"In a way, yes. He raised it up back here a few hundred miles, and I don't consider that he was ever honestly separated from it." This with a withering eye to Durgin.

"It wasn't stolen?"

"It comes to that. He was induced to sell it for one dollar and fifty cents."

For a moment Wilson hesitated and drew back, but it was only a moment. He looked at the bird again. "Well," he said, "I'm not supposed to know that. A bargain's a bargain."

At the moment of being thrust into prominence by the collar, the original owner, somewhat taken by surprise, had mechanically turned up a hand. Now Dalkins seized upon this and held it as in a vice, while Wilson heaped bills upon it till the count should have been lost, though it wasn't. The sum total was two hundred dollars. All the time Durgin had been opening wider and wider at the mouth.

"If I let go," said Dalkins to the original owner, "can I trust you to put that money where it belongs, and not bother me with arguments? Remember it is Christmas, or was a week or so since."

The original owner smiled weakly, but made no remonstrance.

"Where do I come in?" piped up poor Durgin.

"For a good time, and a valuable lesson," snapped Dalkins. "If there's anything else you want but can't seem to lay your hands on, just take it out in kicking."

Then Dalkins gently but forcibly closed the original's fingers over the paper in his hand, and headed him down the aisle. Durgin followed with a rattling in his throat that suggested roup, but merely indicated the impulse to speak without the ability.

Everybody followed, the little procession attracting considerable attention in the hall. It was thought someone had been arrested by a plain clothes man for stealing ribbons from the cages. The original had almost lost consciousness of what was going on around him. He heard as in a dream amid the uproar of roosters, that sounded like a dying yell that wouldn't die, the voice of Dalkins saying, "Go tell that up in the hills, and make them stop breeding mongrel stock."

Editors' Notes

THE texts of Robert Frost's contributions to *The Eastern Poultryman* and *Farm-Poultry* are reproduced herein exactly as originally published, except that typographical errors and certain obvious inconsistencies of editorial handling (as in paragraphing) have been corrected.

The three stories which were included in *The Eastern Poultryman* appeared as follows: "Trap Nests," February 1903, page 71 (with the editor's commentary about the piece on page 72 of the same issue); "A Just Judge," March 1903, pages 89–90; and "A Start in the Fancy," July 1903, pages 147–148.

The nine *Farm-Poultry* appearances were: "A Just Judge" (reprinted from *The Eastern Poultryman*), May 1, 1903, pages 221–222; "The Question of a Feather," July 15, 1903, pages 301–302 (with an editorial note on page 309 referring both to the magazine's original and subsequent consideration of the author's articles); "Old Welch Goes to the Show," August 15, 1903, pages 334–335; "The Original and Only," September 1, 1903, pages 352–353; "Three Phases of the Poultry Industry," December 15, 1903, pages 481–482; "The Cockerel Buying Habit," February 1, 1904, page 54; "'The Same Thing Over and Over,'" March 1, 1904, page 110; "The Universal Chicken Feed," April 1, 1904, page 169; and "Dalkins' Little Indulgence—A Christmas Story," December 15, 1905, pages 513–514.

H. R. White's letter to *Farm-Poultry* and R. F.'s reply, both with appended comments by the editor, were included in the issues of January 15, 1904, page 46, and February

The Eastern Poultryman.

ESTABLISHED 1899 AS THE POULTRYMAN AND POMOLOGIST.

DEVOTED TO PRACTICAL POULTRY CULTURE.

Vol. 4. Freeport, Maine, July, 1903. No. 10.

A Start in the Fancy.

(Written for The Eastern Poultryman.)

The man with the courage of his con-

were common, he believed. They were in the very air of the show room. Scrub birds as scrub prices for scrub buyers, was the cry there, and the imagination of

than as a man with a family he felt equal to.

Still, he was not ready to acknowledge himself beaten. He kept up the fight,

VOL. 16. BOSTON, MASS., DECEMBER 15, 1905. No. 24.

Dalkins' Little Indulgence -- A Christmas Story

IT IS no matter how much Dalkins paid for the bird; the point is that the man who sold it to him somehow got the impression that he did not pay enough -- that he would have paid more. He could not have denied that Dalkins paid him all he asked. So that he had himself to blame if it was not enough. But he got to talking as if he had been cheated—and badly cheated. He enlarged upon the bird until he said he shouldn't wonder if Dalkins would get a cool fifty for it. He groomed it, so to speak, as he thought of it. He made it a little whiter than white, a little more symmetrical than symmetry.

As a matter of fact it was the kind of bird that is worth what one can get for it. It transcended scoring, as it was better than any score reputable judges are willing to sign. It was a bird framed by nature for comparison judging.

If the man who sold it to Dalkins made the mistake of parting with it for a cent less than fifty dollars, he deserved sympathy; but he was the only one who could see that Dalkins deserved blame. He showed himself a poor loser. He talked early and late to all comers about his misfortune that was another man's fault. But almost all comers had been in the same fix themselves, and knew how to make allowances. They did not believe too heartily in the pricelessness of his bird—a suspicion of which made him but talk the more. The wonderful part of this story is that this fellow had picked the bird up away over back in Peacham, Vt., for one dollar and fifty cents. These figures I am willing to vouch for. In that case he did fairly well if he got a five for it. Mind you, I don't say what he got. At the time I heard various rumors. This part of the story must remain shrouded in mystery — men are such liars. I vouch for nothing that you cannot safely believe.

Though he was far enough away from this man and his troubles, the facts here stated somehow or other reached Dalkins. He had come by the bird through an agent or by who had spoiled it by the merest accident from its carriage in passing. He had not been too curious about its history and antecedents at the outset; with him the bird in the hand was the thing. But a certain letter aroused his interest. It was anonymous, doubtless from someone in no way concerned, but bent on mischief making, and informed him that the remarkable bird had been raised by the writer's next door neighbor, and had been started on its career for one dollar and fifty cents. He questioned his agent about it. The agent had heard some such tale. Evidently gossip had been buzzing in the hill town of Peacham. He had heard also that the bird was of the Dalkins strain direct. That was calculated to please Dalkins. He wondered if they couldn't find out who raised it. He would have liked the poor benighted fellow who would part with such a jewel for one fifty to know by its fruits what a thing the Dalkins strain was.

"He didn't suspect what he was doing," he said.

"It isn't likely," said the agent.

"And the fellow who sold him to you?"

"He had some idea, because he's kicking himself for having

sold it. I have seen him since. He is talking at a great rate."

"The bird has made some stir already, then; that's what they call the fatal gift of beauty, isn't it?"

The agent was duly embarrassed. Dalkins was thinking. "Say," he said at last, "I want you to find that original owner and bring him to the New York show on me. And bring the other fellow, too — both of them. I guess I'm good for it. Tell them 'tis a Christmas notion of mine—the show is near enough to Christmas for that. It'll make it easier for you. We'll show them a thing or two, and we'll show the kicker that he only knows a little bit more than the other fellow. And I think I'll show you something. Not a word of this to anyone outside, and not too many words to them.

Just say 'tis my treat — conciliation treat. 'Tis an order." Dalkins' agent found the original owner away over in Peacham one bitter cold morning a day or two after Christmas. Peacham is a New England street town, that is to say, it consists of but one street, which runs north and south along a sharp ridge that looks like the back of a razor backed world. The railroad, when it was built, missed it by about eight miles on the right, and that seemed to send it into a decline—such a close call; no doubt. Many of its fine old houses are going to ruin, and there is never a new one to take their place. The age and size of its shade trees suggested that it might do very well in summer, but on such a day in winter it made the agent fairly groan at the patience of the people

who could abide there. He inquired at the postoffice store for his man, and was sent to the woods for him. He came upon him smoking out logs in a grove recently laid waste, as seriously at work as if he had entirely given up seeing Santa Claus that year. He laid before him his invitation, and while not persuading him on the spot to accept it, succeeded in making him regard it as worth considering. At any rate, he carried him away in triumph from his toil like a Cincinnatus, a Putnam, or a Parker. He left his ox team standing in a brush pile in the care of his fellow workmen.

Before he left he had dinner with him, and it was all arranged. The fellow was a little sheepish at first, as now accused of deliberately circulating counterfeit money—only in this case it would have been a counterfeit bird. He suspected that his punishment was going to take the form of a practical joke. But he decided he was equal to it if only it wasn't to cost him anything, and the return tickets the agent laid down for him set at rest his fears on that score.

The agent had less trouble with the other fellow — Durgin, if the name must out. He considered the invitation his due. "Aw yes," he yawped, "he knew how it all was. Nobody probably intended to do him. It was business, just business. Only he thought," etc. Of course he wasn't a fool. He knew a good bird when he saw one. Only sometimes his mind didn't work quick enough, etc. Yes, he'd be glad to meet Mr. Dalkins. He bore no grudge. He wasn't that kind. Only he thought, etc. The main thing was that he accepted the ticket.

Scene, the New York show. Mr. Dalkins is doing the honors. When I say doing, I mean doing. He never let those two imperfections of his out of his sight for three days, and he never gave them a restful half hour. And it was not all inside the Garden. But let us draw a veil over anything that was irrelevant to the show proper. What have I to do with the Rialto and the Bowery? Suffice it to say that he gave two simple souls the time of their lives, and beat them out in his own enjoyment of it, in spite of the fact that it was on him and it came high.

The grand finale Mr. Dalkins had all prearranged, and he looked forward to it with the anticipation of a boy. No one had an inkling of what was coming, unless it was his agent to whom he once said in an aside: "The bird this bird, was sold, I suppose you didn't know, before anything was placed, but he's not to change hands till the last day of the show. I want you to be there when he does."

And once he had said to the second in line of possession, "So it sticks in your crop that you should have had fifty for your trade. Well, we won't let that spectre intrude on our festivities. Time enough for discussion afterward. There's always a way to settle such matters between gentlemen."

But the victim thought shirking the tone of banter in this, smelt not a rat. He and the original owner came to the final catastrophe as unprepared as the babe new born. They were so absorbed in the pleasure of the hour that it never occurred to either that he might be destined in the mind of the master

Ideal Partridge Cochins.

fifteenth, page 106, respectively, while John A. Hall's letter, actually written by R. F., appeared in the number for March first, page 116.

* * *

The Eastern Poultryman was founded in 1899 as *The Poultryman and Pomologist*, a monthly publication "Devoted to practical poultry and fruit culture." Its change of name occurred with the number for September 1901, and thenceforth the magazine confined its contents to poultry matters only. During the period of R. F.'s contributions it was being issued at Freeport, Maine, with George P. Coffin as editor and publisher. Publication was discontinued in 1905.

Farm-Poultry, a well-established journal in its field, had been started as a monthly in Boston in 1889. Its editor when R. F. contributed to its columns was John H. Robinson, a widely-known figure in poultry circles of that day, and it then appeared bi-weekly. *Farm-Poultry* suspended publication in 1916.

* * *

Of the persons mentioned by R. F. in his article on "Three Phases of the Poultry Industry," the first, Charlemagne Bricault, was born in Canada and was graduated in 1890 as a veterinarian from the Montreal division of Laval University. He earned, also, an additional diploma early the following year from the Ecole de Médecine Vétérinaire de Montréal. He appears in the Lawrence, Massachusetts, city directory in 1894–95, entered as a veterinary surgeon having an office at 303 Common Street and his residence at 53 Cross Street. Late in 1895 Bricault and his wife, Emma, purchased a property in Methuen, Massachusetts, described in its deed as located on the west side of the county road from Lawrence to Salem, New Hampshire, and listed in the Methuen section of the 1896–97 North Andover, Massachusetts, directory as on Prospect Street, near the schoolhouse. This was the farm to which R. F. would have made his visit in the spring of 1899 when exploring the idea of entering upon poultry raising himself.

R. F.'s own temporary residence in Methuen, near Bricault, is documented by a copy of the 1928 edition of his *Selected Poems*, inscribed by the poet "For Charles Bricault from an old Howe Street friend and neighbor named Robert Frost 1929." (Prospect and Howe Streets join in continuation of one another at a point known as Marston Corner, in the northern section of Methuen.)

The Bricaults continued in Methuen (having, however, the Lawrence Post Office as a mail address) until 1900. The Bricault Farm's advertisements in *Farm-Poultry* during the latter part of this period—each carrying the standard headline "bred-to-lay"—reflect an evident shift of concentration from dealing in both Barred Plymouth Rocks and White Wyandottes to White Wyandottes alone. The former are not mentioned in insertions after September 1, 1899.

Following the October 15, 1900, number of *Farm-Poultry*, Doctor Bricault's regular advertisements discontinued, and on December first the magazine's "News Notes" columns (page 435) announced, "Dr. C. C. Bricault, formerly in charge of the Bricault Poultry Farm, at Lawrence, Mass., goes to Maplewood Farm, Woodstock, Vt., where he will have charge of the poultry, and where under his management the proprietor of Maplewood Farm intends to make its poultry plant and stock second to none. Dr. Bricault takes a part of his stock with him. He has F.-P.'s best wishes for success in his new venture."

The Vermont association proved short-lived, however, and beginning with the *Farm-Poultry* issue for August 15, 1901 (page 342), Bricault is again found offering to the poultry-buying public his "Bred-to-lay White Wyandottes," giving his new location as Andover, Massachusetts. (On the facing page of this same number, J. Foster Rhodes, as he had done in the previous issue as well, advertised his Maplewood Poultry and Dairy Farm for sale.) On September fifteenth *Farm-Poultry* included among its "News Notes" (page 372) the report that, "Dr. C. Bricault has resumed business for himself, having located in Andover, Mass. He will continue breeding the same stock along the same lines pursued before he went to Maplewood Farm. He says a year as manager has convinced him that an independent business is more satisfactory, and he is in it now for himself and to stay. He invites correspondence from all his former customers and all interested in bred-to-lay stock."

The Registry of Deeds for northern Essex County, Massachusetts, (located at Lawrence) contains evidence of the Bricaults' acquisition of a four-and-one-half-acre farm in Andover on August 7, 1901, and the mortgage sale of the Methuen property on November twenty-sixth of that same year. (Other vicissitudes in the title to the Methuen farm are traceable in the volumes of the Lawrence Registry office.) Local directories give the Bricaults' Andover address as 64 Salem Street.

From 1906 through 1908 Doctor Bricault is entered again in the Lawrence directory as a veterinarian, practicing at 554 Common Street, but with his residence given as Andover. It is possible that this renewal of practice in Lawrence coincided with an abandonment or curtailment of the Doctor's poultry business. In 1909, as recorded by the city directory, the Bricaults were back living in Lawrence once more, Emma Bricault being listed as engaging in dressmaking at their home at 934 Essex Street. The county Registry records a foreclosure on their Andover farm on April 1, 1909.

The dates cited in the preceding paragraph are of interest, also, in connection with R. F. As has been noted, he became a member of the Pinkerton Academy faculty in the fall of

111

1906. Subsequently, during 1910, he moved from his farm into Derry Village, near the Academy. In an obvious reference to Bricault, R. F. once told an interviewer, "I sold my eggs to a man who bred White Wyandottes. For a while I was fairly well off until he went out of business. He became a horse doctor in Haverhill." (*The Christian Science Monitor*, March 8, 1963, page 9.) It is known that R. F. continued in the poultry business himself only a short time after Bricault ceased to provide a market for his eggs.

Charlemagne Bricault moved to Haverhill, Massachusetts, in 1910, and the Haverhill directory for that year records him as practicing at F. C. Newcomb's Stable, 27 Fleet Street, and at the Central Club Stable on Central Street in the Bradford district. The following year, 1911, he is indicated as making his headquarters at 9 Stage Street, and the next number of the directory enters 19 Main Street as his business address. His residence in the years 1910–13 was 86 Chestnut Street. The Registry of Deeds for southern Essex County, at Salem, gives May 6, 1913, as the date of purchase of the property at 1 Twelfth Avenue, which was to be Doctor Bricault's home for the remainder of his life.

On January 1, 1912, Bricault became Milk Inspector in Haverhill, a post he held until his retirement in April 1939. He died a decade later, on January 10, 1949, aged eighty-two. An obituary notice carried on that date by the *Haverhill Evening Gazette* makes mention, among other things, of the Doctor's prominence as a breeder of Boston terriers, but gives no information about his poultry-raising activity or the history of his earlier years, in Lawrence, Methuen, Woodstock, and Andover.

*   *   *

John Amos Hall was born and died in the little town of Atkinson, New Hampshire, although in the poem "New Hampshire" (first published in 1923) R. F., for poetic purposes, wrote of him as coming instead from Windham:

> When I left Massachusetts years ago
> Between two days, the reason why I sought
> New Hampshire, not Connecticut,
> Rhode Island, New York, or Vermont was this:
> Where I was living then, New Hampshire offered
> The nearest boundary to escape across.
> I hadn't an illusion in my hand-bag
> About the people being better there
> Than those I left behind. I thought they weren't.
> I thought they couldn't be. And yet they were.
> I'd sure had no such friends in Massachusetts
> As Hall of Windham, Gay of Atkinson,
> Bartlett of Raymond (now of Colorado),
> Harris of Derry, and Lynch of Bethlehem.

Atkinson is situated along the Massachusetts line, just east of Salem, New Hampshire, and adjacent to the southeast tip of Derry.

At his death on December 16, 1906, (at the age of sixty-one years, eleven months, and sixteen days) Hall, a bachelor, left a meagre estate indeed. But it was, as is apparent from an inventory in the files of the Rockingham County Probate Office at Exeter, New Hampshire, a poultryman's estate withal—a full third of the appraised value of Hall's personal property being represented by nine geese and a total of one hundred and five hens.

John Hall's competitive success as an exhibitor at poultry shows is attested not only by R. F.'s own account, but by a number of surviving published references as well. His triumphs, for example, at the Amesbury, Massachusetts, show, the site of his first meeting with R. F. and the place their friendship began, are recorded as follows in 1899 in *The Poultryman and Pomologist* for December (page 26): "Mr. J. A. Hall, Atkinson, N. H., was present with some fine White Wyandottes, geese, ducks, etc. winning on White Wyandottes, 1; cockerel, 2, 3; pullet, 1; pen, 1; Embden Geese, 1; old pair, 1; young Pekin Ducks, 1; Black Austrian Ducks, best pair, 1 drake, 1 duck. These are a novelty, being as large as the Pekin, of very quiet disposition, of early maturity, and jet black in color." The following year, 1900, Hall was not only included among Amesbury's award winners in the White Wyandotte group, but also received the forty-dollar "sweepstakes cup," presented to the "exhibitor showing the largest number of birds of one variety scoring over 90 points" (*Farm-Poultry*, January 1, 1901, page 22).

The achievements of the Hall geese at Lawrence, mentioned in the letter written by R. F. to *Farm-Poultry* but published over Hall's signature (March 1, 1904, page 116), is in reference to the Lawrence Poultry, Pigeon and Pet Stock Association's 1903 show, held at the City Hall on December eighth through twelfth of that year.

*   *   *

The "Mr. Nichols" of Salem, New Hampshire, also treated by R. F. in his article on "Three Phases of the Poultry Industry" was evidently Frank H. Nichols, a native of Lawrence, Massachusetts, who is listed in the Lawrence city directory throughout the period 1885 to 1891–92, except in the volume for 1887–88, identified as a millwright or carpenter. The Rockingham County Registry of Deeds contains evidence of his having bought property in Salem on January 21, 1893. During later life Nichols ran a small store near Canobie Lake in Salem. He died at Methuen, Massachusetts, on February 2, 1939, aged seventy-five.

*   *   *

Records relative to the title to R. F.'s Derry, New Hampshire, farm in the period 1900–11 are preserved at the Rockingham County Registry in Exeter. The initial transaction is

William P. Frost's purchase of the property on September 25, 1900. Legal notices in *The Derry News* for October 19 and 26, and November 2, 1900, (pages 8, 2, and 6, respectively) also pertain to the acquisition. The announcement of R. F.'s having moved to the farm, made in the October fifth issue of *The Derry News*, appears on the paper's front page in the column headed "Derry Doings."

Conditions of the passage of the property to R. F. from his grandfather's estate are contained in a copy of William P. Frost's will that was entered at the Rockingham County Probate Office in August 1902. The grandfather had died at Lawrence on July 10, 1901.

* * *

Franklane L. Sewell, the artist referred to in R. F.'s poem "A Blue Ribbon at Amesbury," was recognized in his time as probably the world's foremost illustrator of fowl and game birds. Born at Evanston, Illinois, he began his formal art studies at the Chicago Art Institute. He himself once acknowledged his international reputation as a poultry artist with the simple statement, "My biggest success has been with the humble hen." Over a period of many years his strikingly handsome illustrations were prominently featured by poultry journals and other publications in this country, including both *Farm-Poultry* and *The Eastern Poultryman*.

Long a resident of Dayton, Sewell died, aged eighty-one, at nearby Piqua, Ohio, on January 5, 1948.

* * *

The letter to Ernest L. Silver (dated December 8, 1913), quoted from in the introduction, is preserved within the collections of the Dartmouth College Library. That to John T. Bartlett (written, evidently, during mid-March in 1913) is now a part of the Barrett Collection at the Library of the

115

University of Virginia. Charlemagne Bricault's copies of *Selected Poems* (1928) and *A Further Range* (1936), which have been referred to, are currently owned, respectively, by Mr. and Mrs. Harold J. Carrigg of Haverhill, Massachusetts, and by Dartmouth. The texts of R. F.'s inscriptions in these volumes, as well as extracts from the two letters cited, are quoted by consent of the Executor of the Estate of Robert Frost. Brief quotations from the poems "The Housekeeper," "A Blue Ribbon at Amesbury," and "New Hampshire" are made by permission of Holt, Rinehart and Winston, Inc.

*   *   *

Certain of the information contained in the introduction, and not otherwise documented in the above notes, has been drawn from statements made by R. F. in conversations with the editors at various times.